Myopia

Myopia

A Father's Journey into
Love, Loss, and Sight
Beyond Vision

Mohan Ranga Rao

Wellness Writers Press

WELLNESS WRITERS PRESS
An imprint of Pure Ink Press

Paperback ISBN: 979-8-9912047-0-5
Epub ISBN: 979-8-9912047-1-2

First edition by Wellness Writers Press 2025
wellnesswriterspress.com

To my sightless angel, Yogita, who, through her silence, taught me to see with the eyes of the heart, hear the whispers of others' souls, and cherish the blessings we often take for granted. Her brief yet radiant presence remains an eternal light, illuminating my path with gratitude and grace.

This memoir stands as a testament to the profound wisdom she bestowed upon my soul.

CONTENTS

CHAPTER 1

The Weight of Unseen Fears

(June 22, 1989)

L ittle did I know the first blind person I would ever meet would be my four-day-old daughter.

At 7 a.m. on June 22, 1989, a day brimming with promise, I fastened the last button on my crisp, freshly-pressed Christian Dior shirt, smoothing it down before tucking it neatly into my tailored trousers. With a practiced hand, I buckled my belt and, catching my reflection in the mirror, winked at myself with a self-satisfied smirk. The invigorating scent of Paco Rabanne cologne filled the air as I dabbed it onto my skin, the spicy fragrance setting the tone for the day ahead.

As Alan Parsons's "Breakdown" blasted from my CD player, I joined in, belting out the crescendo with the energy only music can evoke. My house in Mysore felt alive, with my voice echoing through the hallways. Whistling as I locked the front door behind me, my footsteps were light on the stone path leading to the gate. Just then, a white Ambassador taxi pulled up, the familiar hum of its engine blending with the morning sounds of birds and distant traffic.

I was thirty-one and had just become a father four days earlier. All my childhood dreams of owning a business, having a family, and living in a house on a hill away from the joint family home where I grew up had become realities.

My two associates from advertising circles, Kishore and Madhu, were waiting in the car. Kishore, recently married, wore a bright white half-sleeve shirt that splendidly matched his fair complexion and dense, black curly hair. Madhu, still a bachelor, wore jeans and a red turtleneck. His beard and glasses gave the misleading impression of a scholar.

I was returning to be with my wife, Mamatha, and our first-born baby at the hospital in Bangalore, about three hours away. While I had stayed there during the actual delivery, anxiously waiting outside the labor ward (because in India, they did not yet allow men inside), I had to return to Mysore the same day to attend to work.

Sunshine burst through the clouds and found me through the taxi window as we set out. The typical roadside scenes, usually objects of my neglect, instead appeared merry. An autorickshaw owner meticulously polished his vehicle while a woman, standing on the sidewalk, washed her face with water from a basin. Flower sellers arranged a variety of blooms in their wooden carts, and a bare-chested muscular man in loose underwear unpacked a sack of ripe coconuts. Simple acts of daily life appeared delightful to me. I basked in the warmth of happiness.

Kishore filled our drive with dirty jokes duly complemented by me, and I laughed so hard I had to use my handkerchief to wipe the tears from my eyes. I did my best to pull myself together, recalling my mother's ominous warning from childhood not to laugh too much at silly things, as something evil would surely follow a fit of prolonged and intense amusement.

As the taxi stopped at Gayatri Hospital, a girl with muddy, disheveled hair tapped on the window, holding a basket full of short jasmine flower garlands to hang over the quintessential Ganesha idol on the dashboard. *Why can't she join a school or something?* I thought, feeling both sorry for her and angry, cursing under my breath as I got out of the vehicle. I gave her a rupee note from my wallet, leaving it to the driver to collect the flower.

"Mohan, we're late," Kishore said. "We will see Mamatha and the baby with you next time."

I nodded and turned toward the hospital entrance, rushing carelessly across the road.

I had not yet been able to hold my daughter in my arms, and now, I was like a little boy eager to play with his first toy car, desperate to pick her up, carry her, stick out my tongue, and watch her reaction as I had done with my fourteen nephews and nieces when they were a few days old. I was full of memories, recalling their wide eyes studying my comical face.

It was around 11 a.m. when I hurried up the entrance steps of the hospital. For the first time, the smell of a healthcare facility—the overarching essence of cheap phenyl—excited me. The door to room eight in the obstetrics ward was ajar, and I minded my steps, tiptoeing inside. Mamatha was sleeping with our daughter nestled between her left arm and bosom. I silently sat next to my wife's feet.

Immersed in the local newspaper, my father-in-law, Ranga Swamy, in his sky-blue half-sleeve shirt and Cots wool trousers, was seated on a plastic chair. He noticed me, nodded his head, and returned to reading. My mother-in-law, Leela, was sitting on the cot wearing a green cotton saree and a matching blouse, staring at the mosaic-tiled floor with her hands resting on her thighs. She looked at me and smiled.

A cool monsoon breeze whispered through the rusty window grill. I rose quietly, drew the curtains shut, and returned to my seat. The room settled into a serene stillness, punctuated only by the rhythmic hum of the ceiling fan. Minutes later, my daughter stirred in Mamatha's arms, letting out a soft whimper—a delicate newborn sound that seemed to fill the space.

Mamatha's eyelids fluttered open.

I stood and moved closer to them, drawn by the quiet miracle of the moment.

"When did you arrive?" she whispered.

"Just a few minutes ago," I replied.

"You drove?"

"No. I came in a taxi with Madhu and Kishore."

"Where are they? Didn't they want to see the baby?" she asked, perplexed.

"No, they couldn't come today, my dear. They were in a hurry."

My baby's color had changed from brownish-red to pink and white. I reached down to gently caress her surprisingly thick hair, then delicately opened her tiny, clenched fist with my fingers. She clasped my forefinger tightly, sending a surge of thrill through me. My baby's little hand around my finger felt more intimate than a warm hug. For the first time, I experienced a new and unique sense of bonding. I suddenly felt a lot more like an adult, with an emotional heaviness of responsibility, as if I had developed a new extra organ that demanded my love and care. It seemed like a pink and rosy angel had been sent to make a man out of me.

Our baby started to move her hands and legs, but her eyes were closed. I snapped my fingers. She opened her eyes briefly without focusing on my face and closed them again. I whistled gently, and she moved her head. Her eyes remained closed this time.

I snapped my fingers again and bent down to whisper into her ear, "Hello, my pretty little angel."

She still did not open her eyes.

"Why isn't she opening her eyes?" I questioned, half to myself and half to the others in the room, still looking at my baby. I asked my mother-in-law, who was now sitting next to Mamatha, caressing her, "What color are her eyes? Hazel like Mamatha's or dark brown like mine?"

She looked at her husband.

I looked at him, too.

My father-in-law was dead quiet.

Finally, Leela mumbled with a shaky voice, "She has not opened her eyes fully. Sometimes, it can take a couple of days for a newborn to open their eyes, Mohan." She avoided looking at me, which was not unusual, but something was not right about her avoidance this time, since my father-in-law had not said a word.

I sensed the silence that followed was more awkwardness than indifference. I looked at Mamatha and saw tears rolling down her cheeks from her large hazel eyes. "What's the matter, Mamatha? Why are you crying?"

She shook her head vigorously. "She is not opening her eyes fully, Mohan. They say she may have an eye problem, and it will take three to four days for the ophthalmologist to make a proper diagnosis. But she is fine in all other Apgar tests."

Her words pierced my heart like a sickle through the thick shell of a coconut. A strong current surged to my forehead and spread through the back of my head to my spine. I knew an Apgar score evaluated a newborn baby's health, and I was relieved to hear she was fine in those parameters, but what was wrong with her eyes? "What? What problem?" I asked hoarsely as my mouth became dry.

"My Uncle Jayee visited us and told us babies can have conjunctivitis at birth and it can take a couple of days to open their eyes fully," Mamatha replied.

Jayee was the nickname for Dr. Jayaprakash, Mamatha's maternal uncle and a practicing physician. Again, an eerie silence. I looked at my father-in-law, desperately wanting to know more.

Ranga Swamy pinched his nose with his left hand in his characteristically contemplative style, and at last said, "Don't get worked up, Mohan. There is nothing to worry about. Some babies take a little longer to focus on others' faces."

Given my mind's tendency to catastrophize, I started picturing worst-case scenarios. *What if my child has a major vision problem?!*

I got up and started pacing around the room like a bear in a cage. "I would like to speak to Dr. Jayaprakash right away. Can I please have his number?" I picked up the pen and notepad next to the bed.

After a brief silence, Leela softly said his number.

I looked up at her with a strained look on my face.

She cleared her throat and repeated the number louder for me.

I hurried out and called the number from the front desk.

"Dr. Jayaprakash's clinic," answered the receptionist on the other end.

"My name is Mohan. I am the husband of Dr. Jayaprakash's niece, Mamatha. I need to talk to him urgently."

"Hold on a minute." She put me on hold as a contrived electronic tune banged in my ears. A moment later, she returned. "He's seeing a patient right now. Can he call you back in five minutes?"

I provided the appropriate number to have them call me back, then hung up. My tension receded only slightly since surely he would have taken my call if there was an immediate worry. I sat on the chair across from the front desk, despite my aversion and allergy to plastic. The smell of phenyl was reduced, but now repelled me.

The phone rang after ten minutes, and the lady at the front desk picked it up, listened for a few seconds, and nodded at me.

I got up and grabbed the receiver. "Hello, Dr. Jayaprakash. This is Mohan. I arrived just now from Mysore. I am worried about my daughter not opening her eyes even after four days. Do you know what's wrong?" I pleaded.

"Hello, Mohan. Please don't be worried. I saw your baby at the hospital and spoke with Mamatha. Your daughter looks to be doing fine," he tried to reassure me.

"Then why have they sought an ophthalmologist's opinion?"

"Dr. Kannan feels the baby's eyes need a routine check by an eye specialist to rule out conjunctivitis."

"Will she be able to see me?" My voice was jittery.

"Of course, of course. I will come and see you at Leela's house this evening. You are going back to your in-laws' home this afternoon, right?"

I replied that we were, and then we hung up. I returned to the room, less anxious but still in a state of shock.

"Did you speak to Jayee?" Mamatha asked, sitting upright on the bed as she fed the baby.

"Yes. Your uncle told me there was nothing to worry about and that she might have mild conjunctivitis. He will visit us at your parents' tonight." I sat down on the bed next to Mamatha.

Just then, our esteemed obstetrician, Dr. Kannan, entered our room. She put her white coat over her saree and a stethoscope around her neck.

Ranga Swamy got up, and I followed suit.

"Ah, you are a lucky father. Congratulations! Your daughter is very beautiful. I conducted the Apgar test. She is quite healthy."

Without bothering to exchange pleasantries, I said, "I'm curious why you advised an eye exam for her," hoping she might have more details to offer me.

Sensing my concern, she calmly replied, "I've advised a routine examination to determine if any intervention is needed. You should take your child as soon as possible."

Her last sentence sent a surge of distress through my body once again. It felt more grave than what Jayee had said. The weight of unseen fears consumed my thoughts while the others in the room remained unperturbed. Why was everyone being so casual about this? I was perplexed. But I knew I had to stay calm for Mamatha's sake.

Pulling myself together with all my strength, I managed to thank Dr. Kannan as she left to see her other patients. My chest tightened with the uncertainty ahead, yet my nerves slowly settled as I turned back to Mamatha. She smiled at me, her face glowing despite the strain of birth and the few days since.

Why am I worrying? I am the luckiest man alive, married to the most incredibly beautiful woman, and now, a father to our precious daughter.

As I watched her cradle our baby, my thoughts drifted to the day I stood before the altar, waiting for Mamatha to become my wife. That day, too, I had been filled with the same mix of anxiety and hope. Just as we had embarked on that new journey together, now, as parents, we were stepping into an even greater one—uncertain, yes, but one we would face side by side.

CHAPTER 2

The Eyes of Destiny

(December 1987 - November 1988)

The morning air was crisp, seeping into my room despite the closed windows, wrapping around me like a cool blanket. I was lying back on my bed, propped up against a pillow, legs stretched out, a lit cigarette lazily perched between my fingers. The faint wisps of smoke spiraled up toward the ceiling as I thumbed through the pages of *Jonathan Livingston Seagull* by Richard Bach. The peaceful solitude of the moment was interrupted by a soft, almost tentative knock on my bedroom door.

It had been four long months since the explosive family dispute with my brother, Murthy, and the rift still hung heavy in the air. Tired of not feeling valued, my mind was already on a different path—preparing to leave our ancestral home, Sita Vilas, and setting my sights on marriage and a future away from the tangled web of family conflicts.

Despite the lingering tensions, Sulochana, my eldest sister-in-law, finally felt it was time to search for a bride for me, following the tradition of arranged marriages in India. She had been married to my brother, Guru, since I was just eight years old and had become more of a mother figure to me than a sister-in-law. I called her "Athige," a respectful term in Kannada, my mother tongue, as addressing her by name would have felt improper.

The familiar sound of her voice broke the silence as she stepped into the room. "Moni, do you want to meet this girl and see if you like her and maybe even marry her?" She clutched a photograph between her fingers, fluttering it gently as it carried the weight of the decision ahead.

About three years earlier, when I had requested Sulochana's help in finding a girl for me to marry, she had laughingly replied, "But your older brother, Sridhar, is not yet married." I had kept quiet, but now that Sridhar was married, the time was finally right.

I stubbed out my cigarette in the ashtray, setting aside the book, and got up to meet her. We both sat down on the edge of the bed, and I took a closer look at the photograph of a girl wearing a saree, posing awkwardly in front of the camera.

As I studied the image, she stroked my arm affectionately and said, "Moni, her name is Mamatha. She's beautiful and a good girl, trust me."

After taking a moment to contemplate, I replied, "Please give me a few days, Athige," and handed her back the photo. I wasn't impressed with what I saw—an old-fashioned girl posing awkwardly in front of the camera. Clad in a dull saree with no makeup, she looked like a typical bourgeois damsel, content with the mundane and mediocre.

"I'll set up a meeting, Moni," Sulochana said with maternal eagerness.

"Okay, Athige, if you say so." I agreed out of respect for her.

As the matriarch of our large joint family, Sulochana arranged for Mamatha's family to visit Mysore and set up a meeting at Sita Vilas for the 25th of December, 1987, the following Saturday.

At around 10 a.m. that day, I watched through the large windows of the upstairs foyer as an auto-rickshaw arrived outside our family compound. A fair, lean, middle-aged man with a slight paunch got off the rickshaw in the company of a hefty woman and a pretty, slender girl in a saree. They entered through the front gate.

I went downstairs and joined Guru and Sulochana, who were welcoming the girl's family inside. The potential bride-to-be, her father, and her mother took their seats in the drawing room while I sat directly across from the girl. The only part of her I could see was her scalp, as she kept her head down.

She sat like a frightened dove, with the half dozen kids of Sita Vilas taking turns to come close and peek at her. About twenty of us who lived at Sita Vilas, spanning all age groups, hovered around like vultures circling a lamb, stealing glances at her.

After about thirty minutes into our meeting, Sulochana spoke up. "Mamatha, don't you want to look at Mohan?"

Mamatha finally lifted her head and looked at me for a few seconds. Her face was oval and symmetrical.

I saw beautiful, large hazel eyes. I had never seen more beautiful eyes in my life.

They were the eyes of destiny, and I melted. Even today, as I write these words, whenever I try to read Mamatha's eyes, I feel the same way I did when we first met—completely mesmerized by their beauty, forgetting everything else.

Mamatha's parents and my eldest brother spent another half hour discussing my business and our families. They left without giving me a chance to talk to Mamatha alone.

A couple of days later, Mamatha's father called Guru to ask for my answer, and Guru, in turn, asked for my opinion.

"But has the girl agreed?" I asked.

Sulochana, who was sitting next to Guru, smiled and said, "He called because the girl likes you, Moni."

"But Athige," I said, "she didn't utter a single word. I'd like another meeting with only her before I give my answer, please."

So, she set up a meeting between the two of us for January 3, 1988, in Bangalore, where my sister, Vanaja, lived. The memory of this meeting is still vivid in my mind. I was upstairs, leafing through *Reader's Digest* when my sister called out to me from downstairs.

Smiling teasingly, Vanaja said, "She's here. What's her name, Mona?"

"Mamatha," I replied, rolling my eyes, then went to meet her.

Mamatha sat in the foyer with her father.

I shook her father's hand and took the chair next to his.

"I'll be inside. You two can talk," Mamatha's father said, then left, gently closing the double doors to the living room behind him.

The nineteen-year-old girl who sat on the edge of the large bamboo chair with her hands folded in her lap, instead of resting on the armrests, made me smile inwardly. She wore an orange saree, and her arms were so thin I could see her protruding elbow bones. She was staring at the floor, and for several seconds, we both just listened to the ticking of the wall clock.

I cleared my throat, and then, appearing shy and nervous, she looked at me. Her eyes were so captivating I could only stare into those hazel masterpieces. I forgot my words. Finally gathering myself, I asked, "How are you?"

In a shaky, slightly husky tone, she replied, "Fine," and for the first time, I heard her voice.

"I know you're in your final year of B. Com at NMKRV College. What does NMKRV stand for?"

"That's the short form for my college name," she said, her voice quivering with nervousness, "Nagaratnamma Meda Kasturi Ranga Shetty Rashtriya Vidyalaya." By the time she finished the last word of her school's name, she had run out of breath.

I was surprised by the somewhat thick, masculine quality of her voice. "Do you want a glass of water?"

She nodded.

I went inside, fetched a glass of water, and offered it to her.

She tossed her head back and looked up at me with her angelic eyes.

I collapsed back in my chair. "Are you aware I am almost ten years older than you?"

"Yes," she replied.

"Are your parents forcing you to marry me?"

She shook her head vigorously, like a schoolgirl.

"Do you know I'm in charge of new small businesses that are struggling to sustain and grow?"

She cocked her head slightly, again reminding me of the age gap between us.

"I can take care of all our financial needs; you don't have to worry," I said, parroting the advice of one of my elders.

"I'm sure our businesses will all flourish and grow," Mamatha said shyly.

Hearing her say, "our businesses," and knowing someone believed in me, I felt a mild elation. Curious, I asked, "How can you be so sure?"

"I'm considered the lucky charm of our family. My father believes it was only after I was born that he began to see prosperity."

"Hmm," I nodded, as though her answer had addressed my doubts. I envied her optimism, which stemmed from her secure and uncynical upbringing—a stark contrast to mine, where rivalry and one-upmanship among us brothers had been our main emotional nutrients.

Culturally speaking, it felt like an affair between beauty and the beast, and before I knew it, our visit was over.

Later that day, I told Sulochana I liked Mamatha and would like to marry her. After both families agreed to tie the knot, our *lagna patrika*—the engagement—was set for April 4, 1988, with the wedding to follow in July. Anticipating my opportunity to leave our family home, I chose a two-bedroom house in Gokulam, in the western part of Mysore, and signed on to a long lease at 3,000 Rupees per month (approximately 35 USD per month). I didn't bother informing my brothers or my sisters-in-laws about this arrangement, as I knew they wouldn't like it.

Within a few weeks of meeting, I took Mamatha to dinner at the Taj West End Hotel on our first date. While I smoked, some of the smoke blew into her face, making her cough. I quickly put out the cigarette and promised to quit soon. Her smile gave me the push I needed, and the very next day, I stopped for good.

As our relationship progressed, Mamatha introduced me to her relatives, and I accompanied her to buy 1,000 banana leaves for the wedding lunch and to see the garlands for the decorations. Most Indian weddings are a matter of great joy that keep the women in the extended family occupied for several months, bringing them together for the family function. Our wedding was going to be a two-day affair and would involve *Vara Pooja* (welcoming the groom), *Kanyadaan* (giving away the bride), *Sapthapadhi* (the seven-step oath), and the tying of the *mangalsutra* (a holy matrimonial chain) around the bride's neck.

Even though I was born into a large multigenerational family with deep loyalty to Hindu culture and spent my childhood partaking in many Hindu festivities and rituals, I never truly had much reverence for or loyalty to them. As a result, my disdain for tradition and rituals robbed me of the anticipatory joy I imagined to be customary before a wedding. For our wedding, I secretly wished I could fast-forward through the upcoming function like we did while watching boring videos.

Mamatha's parents chose Nijaguna Banquet Hall for the wedding rituals in Bangalore, where my bride-to-be lived with them, about 140 kilometers from Mysore. The *Vara Pooja* was scheduled for the evening of July 7. Five of my brothers, two sisters, their spouses, and twenty-one nephews and nieces left for Bangalore in the afternoon and arrived around 7 p.m. My sixth brother, Murthy, did not join us, as I had stopped speaking to him a year earlier because of our falling out. I was welcomed with the traditional *Aarthi* (a ritual in which a small flame is circled around the face), which suddenly made the reality of my marriage sink in.

That night, I lay awake for hours, thinking about the life ahead. I was getting married the next day, yet uncertainty clouded my thoughts—our family business was in the midst of a partition, and I wasn't sure of my role. I was also marrying a sweet, innocent girl still in her final year of college, and the importance of that responsibility, combined with the worries over my business ventures, felt overwhelming. I feared the businesses I had started might crumble under the strain of our family dispute.

But each time I thought of Mamatha, my anxiety faded, replaced by dreams of a future filled with romance, happiness, and joy. Her goodness gave me hope.

The next morning, well before the sun was up, my aunt Parimala knocked on my door, waking me for the rituals set to begin at 6 a.m. A junior priest helped me put on a silk *dhoti*—a rectangular piece of pure white silk cloth, around twelve feet long—that wrapped around my waist and legs and knotted at the waist, with a fold that went between my legs. A red silk rectangular cloth with golden borders covered my shoulders and chest.

As I approached the wedding altar, my silk dhoti started to slide down, and my cousin, Chandru, had to bring a jute thread and tie it tightly around my waist. I climbed the five steps to the dais where the marriage rituals would take place; people were already gathering in the seating area.

In my culture, boys used to be sent to a *gurukula* at age seven or eight to study the Vedas and spiritual texts for twelve years, fostering detachment from worldly life. This study often inspired them to move to the sacred city of Kashi. The *Kashi Yatra* ritual symbolizes this tradition, where the bride's father symbolically stops the groom from leaving for Kashi, washes his feet, and requests him to marry his daughter.

After the poojas and rituals intended solely for me were complete, Mamatha entered the hall, her presence captivating, draped in a rich peacock-blue saree with a vibrant red border. The shimmering fabric glowed under the soft light of the ceremonial lamps. Her beauty surpassed anything I had ever envisioned, even more radiant than in my wildest dreams. The intricate designs of her saree, paired with the grace in her step, made her seem almost otherworldly.

As the priest tied her saree to my dhoti, symbolizing the sacred bond of our union, I was overwhelmed by an unexpected sense of triumph. In that moment, it felt like I had won something rare and precious. By 7:30 a.m., I tied the mangalsutra around Mamatha's neck—a delicate gold chain, its black beads glistening against her skin—signifying to the world that she was now my wife. The three knots I tied symbolized the eternal bond of our souls, a promise that we would be united for the rest of our lives.

I gently took Mamatha's hand, feeling her slight tremor, and guided her as she touched seven betel nuts with her right toe. All the while, the Hindu priest's rhythmic chanting filled the air, reciting the sacred seven vows in flowing Sanskrit from the Vedas. Seven married women from Mamatha's family gathered around her, their whispers of blessings in her right ear floating like soft melodies. This ceremony, known as *Sapthapadhi*, the seven steps, was the heart of our wedding— symbolizing more than the joining of two individuals—merging our two destinies, sealed by timeless ritual.

Throughout the wedding, my eldest brother, Guru, and his wife, Sulochana, assumed the role of my parents and went to great lengths to ensure everything went smoothly.

After all the rituals had concluded, Mamatha and I stood at the wedding reception for three long hours, greeting guests and receiving their blessings. By the time the event wound down, it was nearly 10 p.m. The experience was grueling, especially for Mamatha, who stood beside me in her vibrant wedding saree, weighed down by heavy jewelry—green bangles adorning her wrists, diamond rings on her fingers, silver toe rings, a golden armlet, and a golden waistband. Under the heat of the lights, her exhaustion was palpable.

I couldn't wait to whisk her away to the Sheraton Hotel, where Guru and Sulochana had made arrangements for our nuptial night. The drive there felt endless. Once we arrived in our room, the sight of the floral decorations on the bed and the sweet, intoxicating scent filling the room mesmerized me. Mamatha's wrists jingled with six pairs of colorful bangles—red, green, and yellow—which made an alluring sound every time she moved her hands. By tradition, the bride wears these bangles as part of her wedding makeup, but by the next morning, the delicate glass bangles were scattered about the room, a silent testament to our incredible first night together.

Mamatha and I were to leave for our new house the next morning. Contrary to the traditional Hindu belief that a bride sheds tears when leaving her parents' home, Mamatha did not shed a single drop as we headed to our new home together.

According to an age-old Hindu custom known as *Griha Pravesh*, to usher in wealth and happiness, requires a new daughter-in-law to step on a pot of rice at the entrance of her husband's home. At Sita Vilas, my six sisters-in-law awaited Mamatha's arrival with a jar of rice, expecting us to visit before moving to our new house. When we bypassed Sita Vilas and went directly to our new home, they drove six kilometers to join us and set up the formalities.

Sulochana, disapproving, said, "You should have informed us about moving into your new house, Moni."

I avoided her gaze and mumbled an apology.

The other sisters-in-law voiced their concerns about my independence and estrangement from the family.

"Please, stop chastising me in front of my new wife," I pleaded, as Mamatha remained silent.

Sulochana then lightened the mood by drawing a Rangoli at the entrance.

Mamatha performed the Griha Pravesh ritual by toppling the vessel of rice and entered the house, followed by my sisters-in-law, who helped us arrange our belongings for an hour or so. The house, which had been empty for months, needed cleaning. While Mamatha swept and mopped, I set up the furniture, music system, and TV. Exhausted, we collapsed onto the new brown sofa, finally alone and content.

"So, we're on our own, Mamatha," I said cheerfully.

She nodded enthusiastically.

"You know, I've dreamt of this day ever since my childhood."

"What do you mean, Mohan?"

"To have a home and family of my own."

Mamatha looked thoughtful as she listened to me, then said, "Sulochana gave me an expensive saree and told me to wear it at our second wedding reception tomorrow." She leaned back on the sofa and shut her eyes. "And you know what she told me?"

"No. What?"

"'Take care of Moni for me and love him all you can. He needs to be loved,'" Mamatha said softly.

I was pleasantly surprised and secretly happy my sister-in-law cared so much about me.

The second wedding reception, held on the 10th of July in Mysore, was a grand affair for over 3,000 guests from all over India. With twenty food carts and a striking ice sculpture featuring "M&M" (Mamatha and Mohan), it quickly became the talk of the town.

Afterward, Mamatha and I spent three days unpacking and savoring our new life together in our own home while indulging in each other's company. We made love several times a day and were thoroughly absorbed in each other.

Our honeymoon followed, which was a week-long trip to Ooty and Kodaikanal. The Savoy experience was vintage, offering a colonial-era ambiance with afternoon high tea, croquet on the lawns, spa sessions, and scotch by the fireplace. Though we had the chance to enjoy these amenities, our preoccupation with each other meant we barely left our room. On the rare occasion that we did, I managed to row a romantic wooden boat along the lake's perimeter and sing "Jo Tumko" to Mamatha, which she adored.

Despite the delightful honeymoon, we were eager to return to our new home and start our life together. For the first time in our lives, Mamatha and I lived by ourselves. It was a foreign but liberating feeling as we were both so used to having many people around us at all times. In fact, for the first four months, we also had no domestic help, and Mamatha managed the house entirely on her own. At just twenty years old and having recently completed her degree in commerce, she found it challenging to cook and clean, but she refused to hire any help.

"I'm sorry, Mamatha. I'm trying to find someone who can at least wash the dishes and clean the house," I told her one day.

She shrugged it off, and I couldn't help but feel a surge of pride for her resilience.

I spent the best four months of my life at our Gokulam house. Our intimacy was a joyful highlight, enveloping us in a cocoon of closeness.

One evening in October 1988, I returned home from work feeling exhausted. It was around 6:30 p.m., and as I walked in, I saw Mamatha holding a Barbie doll and combing its lustrous blonde hair.

"Where in the world did you get that?" I asked, astonished by her new hobby.

"I bought it. I love combing girls' hair."

"Whatever makes you happy," I said with a shrug.

"Mohan, can we go out for some samosa masala?" she asked, looking up with a smile.

"Sure," I said, grabbing my car keys from the table.

We had driven less than a few hundred feet when Mamatha suddenly said, "Mohan, I'm expecting a guest," while straightening her hair.

"Oh? Your dad or mom?" I asked.

"Actually, I was expecting this guest, but wasn't sure until today. Any other guesses?"

I shook my head.

She looked somewhat disheartened.

I tried again. "Your brother, Rajiv?"

She sighed deeply at my failure to guess, then said softly,

"I'm pregnant."

CHAPTER 3

My First Glimpse of Life as a Father

(November 1988 - June 18, 1989)

I slammed the brakes with such force that a small pillow from the back seat shot forward, landing between us with a soft thud. The tires screeched against the road as I pulled over to the side. My fingers fumbled with the key as I turned off the engine.

"You're pregnant?" The words flew out of my mouth, my voice a few octaves higher than usual, revealing my shock and excitement.

Mamatha tilted her head slightly, her lips curling into a soft, knowing smile. In that instant, the realization hit me like a wave—soon, I would be a father. A flood of emotions—pride, exhilaration, and disbelief—swept over me. I blinked, trying to steady myself as the reality sank deeper.

"Wow," I finally managed, pressing my tongue against the inside of my right cheek, struggling to contain the emotions swirling inside me. I didn't want to lose my composure, but my excitement, bubbling beneath the surface, threatened to spill over.

With a sudden burst of energy, I twisted the key in the ignition and revved the engine back to life. "Yes!" I shouted, my triumphant cry echoing through the car, my worries dissolving into thin air. A strange sense of relief washed over me. It was as if the impact of an unspoken concern had finally lifted: the irrational fear that my past masturbation habits had somehow affected my fertility.

When I glanced over at Mamatha and saw her face glowing with joy and calmness, I decided to celebrate. I took her to her favorite spot, Chic-Chic-Tha, a bustling little restaurant known for its Mumbai-style street food. The aroma of fried spices and tangy chutneys filled the air as we sat down, and I ordered her favorite golgappas—crispy puff-pastry balls stuffed with spiced mashed potatoes, tangy water, and tamarind juice.

After indulging in our Mumbai-style chaats, we shared ice cream from the same cup.

As soon as we got home, I called my brother Sridhar to share the news.

"Congrats, Mona. Nanda is expecting too," he said.

"Congrats, Sri," I replied. We decided to meet and celebrate together.

The first few weeks of Mamatha's pregnancy were normal, but she did experience daily nausea for most of it and craved spicy and sour foods. Her mother sent us a bottle of lime pickles, loaded with red chili powder, to satisfy her cravings.

Two months into her pregnancy, I opened the bottle of pickles for our lunch. I served a piece to each of us and was surprised to see Mamatha eating straight from the bottle, licking her fingers, and reaching back for more. I was shocked and a bit concerned for her health. She had devoured an entire 300-gram jar of spicy lime pickles in one sitting and acted as if she had just had ice cream.

By her fourth month, as I was packing for a business trip to Mumbai, Mamatha approached me. "Mohan, could you please buy knitting needles and four big bundles of red wool and one bundle of white wool while you're there? I want to knit a red sweater with white borders for the baby."

"Of course. Is your aunt coming to visit you tomorrow?"

"Yes. I'm looking forward to it."

Mamatha had an aunt who was studying gynecology and had come to Mysore on vacation. She wanted to see how Mamatha was coping with her pregnancy and provide her with a free examination. However, during the internal examination the next day, her aunt inadvertently applied too much pressure. Mamatha returned home in significant pain and only called me the following day. "Mohan, can you come home, please? I don't feel very well."

"What's the matter, Mamatha?" I asked, alarmed.

"I have an unbearable pain in my lower abdomen, and I'm discharging small amounts of blood."

I jumped out of my seat and sped home in my car.

When I arrived, I found Mamatha crying and writhing on the bed. I helped her into the car and rushed her to Kamala Raman Hospital. They quickly took her into the emergency ward, and a female doctor entered the room. I waited anxiously outside.

I started to cry, and despite my best efforts to hold back the sobs, I couldn't. I thought I knew how much I loved Mamatha, but this experience revealed that my love for her was deeper than even I had realized.

Dr. Roopa, the young gynecologist, came out within ten minutes. She had both hands in the pockets of her white coat.

"She's okay," Dr. Roopa said. "But she's just narrowly avoided a threatened miscarriage. She must have strained herself physically. Since it's the first trimester, Mamatha needs complete bed rest. I'll prescribe some medications."

"Could the bleeding have been caused by her examination the other day?" I asked.

Dr. Roopa wasn't keen to comment on that and reiterated the importance of Mamatha taking it easy and not exerting herself.

I decided my wife would not be doing domestic chores from then on.

Dr. Roopa prescribed three different medications and advised Mamatha to take them for six weeks. After a few days in the hospital, and once her bleeding had stopped, I took her to stay with my five brothers and their wives at Sita Vilas. I carried her in my arms from the car to the entrance of Sita Vilas.

I called Dr. Vaidhyanathan, the technical director at Arvee (my new start-up pharmaceutical business), who had become somewhat of a paternal figure to me. As an organic chemist, he was knowledgeable about pharmaceutical drugs.

"Throw all those medicines out, Man. Don't let her take anything," he said, alarmed.

"Why?" I asked, confused.

"It's better to avoid all medications during pregnancy. They might affect the health of the fetus."

However, Mamatha was uncertain about ignoring her gynecologist's advice, so she completed the fifteen-day course.

The next few weeks were uneventful and passed quickly.

In early February of 1988, on a cloudy and gloomy morning, I got up as usual and whispered, "Good morning," in Mamatha's ear.

"Good morning," she replied.

I finished my morning ablutions and was about to leave for my three-mile jog, a routine that I had recently started.

Mamatha was still sitting on the bed and had not gotten up. I assumed she was experiencing morning sickness.

"Is everything okay?" I asked.

She nodded but didn't say anything.

After returning from my jog, I finished my shower and enjoyed the breakfast Mamatha had prepared; Kesari bath, which is a traditional sweet South Indian dish made of semolina, sugar, ghee, and milk, along with my favorite upma, made of cream of wheat, veggies, and spices. I polished off more than my share while Mamatha ate silently.

After breakfast, I took my Maruti Suzuki Gypsy Jeep out of the garage. Mamatha had been unusually quiet all morning, the first time in our nine months of marriage. Suspecting it was a pregnancy thing, I gave her a kiss and left for the office at Arvee as usual. As I reversed my vehicle and passed the gate, I turned to wave at Mamatha, but she wasn't at the door. I shrugged and drove off.

While sorting through the morning correspondence at my office, my secretary, Vasantha, called me on the intercom.

"Sir, Mamatha's father is on the line."

"Connect him," I said, a bit worried, as it was not like him to call me out of the blue. Picking up the phone, I said, "Good morning, Mr. Ranga Swamy."

"Good morning, Mohan. How are you?"

"I'm fine. How are you?"

"Good, good. Listen, do you know what date it is today?"

"Yes, it's the seventh of February. Why?" I asked, still worried.

"What is special about today?"

"I don't know. I can't recall anything special happening today," I said, growing more anxious.

"Can you guess?"

I tried hard but couldn't recall anything significant. "No."

"Today is Mamatha's birthday," he finally blurted out.

"Oh, shit!" After thanking her father for the reminder, I hung up and staggered out of my chair, feeling like I had sunk to the bottom of the deepest ocean. To this day, I have no clue why I forgot her birthday. I left immediately for home.

As I ran through the entrance of our house, calling out for Mamatha, I heard no response. I went to the bedroom and found Mamatha sitting on the bed, crying, her head and hands resting on her knees.

I held her, even as she tried to push me away. It took an hour of cajoling and apologizing to finally convince her to get out of bed and spend the rest of the day with me. When she finally got up, there, on the bed next to her, was a tiny, cute-looking sweater, red with white stripes, and a matching white cap for the baby. It was the smallest, most adorable sweater I had ever seen. For the first time, I could picture our child in my mind. It was my first glimpse of life as a father. From just Mamatha and me, we would soon be a family of three.

This moment of anticipation highlighted the significant cultural expectations surrounding our marriage and parenthood. Traditionally, the burden of prenatal and postnatal care falls on the bride's parents, placing additional responsibilities on them. After our wedding, only Mamatha and I were at our Mysore home. Being six months pregnant, her need for maternal support grew, so Mamatha traveled to Bangalore to stay with her family, adhering to these deep-rooted customs.

Not adept at the nuances of feminine sensibilities, I did not write to Mamatha, even after a week of her departure. Since Mamatha's parents did not yet have a phone at home, I received a call from my father-in-law from his office, informing me that Mamatha was anxious because she hadn't heard from me. From then on, I made it a point to send a postcard every week inquiring about her well-being. She seemed happy with her parents, who were as caring and protective as ever.

My father-in-law called me during Mamatha's seventh month of pregnancy to tell me Mamatha had undergone an ultrasound scan and the results were normal. I felt reassured she was in experienced and safe hands. I visited Mamatha twice a month, and by the time she was eight months pregnant, I could feel the baby kicking from inside her. It was a strange and slightly frightening sensation for me, and I would pull back my hand whenever I felt the baby kick.

As the last month of her pregnancy approached, Mamatha experienced severe back pain and distress most of the time. Finally, on the 18th of June, 1989, while I was at my office at Instant Foods Company, I received a call from my sister-in-law.

"Ranga Swamy called. Mamatha is going into labor. Rush to Bangalore at once, Moni," Sulochana urged.

I left immediately, knowing it would take almost three hours to reach Bangalore.

I was jittery with excitement when I arrived at Gayatri Hospital on Kanakapura Road, where Mamatha had been admitted for her delivery. The maternity center at the hospital was tiny, and I could hear Mamatha screaming as soon as I approached the reception. Both her parents were waiting outside the labor ward. Her father was visibly distressed, almost in tears, unable to bear Mamatha's screams.

"Amma, Anna," her cries continued, each growing more intense. Unable to endure it any longer, my father-in-law went to the entrance of the hospital to wait for the doctor.

Meanwhile, I felt a mix of excitement and happiness, despite the heart-wrenching nature of Mamatha's cries. I knew her distress would soon end with the arrival of our baby.

I imagined her suffering as the storm before the calm. I was accustomed to the noise and chaos of childbirth, having lived in a large Hindu joint family of twenty-one children, spanning from six months to eight years old.

Finally, our obstetrician, Dr. Kannan, arrived. She was in her early thirties and wore a yellow saree and matching blouse under her white coat. She exuded confidence and reliability, which reassured me. Without acknowledging my father-in-law's relieved greetings, she hurried toward the delivery ward. We waited outside for an hour as Mamatha continued to push and cry, screaming in pain every minute. Still, there was no sign of progress in Mamatha's labor.

Dr. Kannan came out still wearing her gloves and said, "I may need to use forceps to pull out the baby's head since her cervix is small."

My father-in-law and I exchanged worried glances. I knew nothing about forceps or deliveries. "Okay, but is there any danger to the baby or to Mamatha?" I asked anxiously.

"No, no. It's very safe," she reassured us. She then wrote down a list of items needed from a pharmacy. In those days, healthcare facilities in India were not integrated, so pharmacies were separate from hospitals for historical and regulatory reasons.

I dashed to the nearby Anuradha Medical Store across the street.

As I re-entered the hospital, I could still hear Mamatha's agonizing screams. My father-in-law was still sobbing in the hallway. I rushed to the delivery ward and handed over the plastic bag with the items Dr. Kannan needed. I then sat beside my father-in-law, trying to offer him some comfort while we anxiously awaited news.

I did not realize then that a forceps delivery, which involves using forceps to gently pull and guide the baby's head from the birth canal, can be associated with significant risks of severe and permanent damage to the baby.

It took another hour before we heard the baby's first wail, precisely at 7:12 p.m. I sighed in relief and shook my father-in-law's hand. Dr. Kannan then took me inside the delivery room. Mamatha was half awake, with the tightly wrapped baby sleeping peacefully beside her. I gently pressed Mamatha's left hand and caressed the baby's cheek with the back of my right palm. I stroked and straightened Mamatha's sweaty hair off of her face, then looked at my baby girl on Mamatha's bosom, my very own creation—my pretty little princess with the sweetest round face.

"I have never seen a baby with such a beautiful complexion. Her face looks like a flower," said Mamatha's mother.

I wanted to hold her in my arms but was afraid of dropping her. I sat next to Mamatha, wanting to speak with her, but the nurse kindly asked me to leave and let her rest.

As I stood to leave, I remarked, "Today is the eighteenth of June. I was born on the eighteenth of January. Like me, my daughter was born on the eighteenth."

Mamatha smiled as I kissed our baby on the forehead. My daughter, with her incredibly beautiful face, slept peacefully. I longed to hold her, but I knew there would be time for that later.

I left the ward overwhelmed with joy and excitement at becoming a father. While a whirlwind filled me with fear, exhilaration, responsibility, and back to fear, my life felt imbued with an immense sense of purpose and significance.

For all of Mamatha's pregnancy, I pictured our healthy child growing, playing, and thriving in the love of our large families. Little did I know, everything I had envisioned for my daughter's life was about to change—in the blink of an eye.

CHAPTER 4

A Future Gone Dark

(June 23, 1989)

Mamatha and our four-day-old baby were discharged in the early afternoon, and we all went to Mamatha's parents' house as planned. Dr. Jayaprakash came by as promised, to provide moral support and comfort that all should be fine with our daughter's eyes. But at the same time, he reaffirmed the importance of our specialist appointment the next morning.

Sridhar, also a doctor, sent word he would arrive in the morning to come with us. And sure enough, by 9 a.m. the following day, the doorbell made its chirping sparrow sound, announcing the arrival of the most endearing of my six older brothers.

"Namaskaara!" he said, greeting my in-laws, who received Sridhar at the entrance.

I felt temporarily elated, emboldened by just one look at my beloved brother, Sridhar, as he reached to remove his shoes. Immaculately dressed in black trousers, a white long-sleeve shirt tucked in, and a leather belt with a shining buckle, his eyes were a little wider than usual. He recognized the anxiety-filled silence in the house. As soon as he entered the living room, he pulled his stethoscope from his briefcase and asked, "Where is Mamatha?"

I took him to the front room where Mamatha was resting and our baby was sleeping in the cradle. Sridhar spent some time checking the baby's reactions to different stimuli. He returned to the living room, and before he sat down, I butted in. "How is she, Sri? Can she see?"

"She looks absolutely healthy and fine," he said, folding his stethoscope.

"Then why have they asked me to take her to Prabha Eye Clinic?"

"Sometimes early intervention will completely resolve any possible vision issues," he said. "If her eyes are infected, they may administer some drops."

I sighed out a deep but shaky breath. To lighten the ambience, Sridhar started talking about the upcoming cricket series and India's chances as we prepared to go to our appointment.

Renowned as one of the top eye clinics in Bangalore in the '80s, Prabha Eye Clinic was thankfully situated just a stone's throw away from Mamatha's parents' home. In fact, Dr. Mehra, one of Bangalore's leading ophthalmologists, was Mamatha's neighbor and someone she respectfully called "Uncle." His son was a close playmate of Mamatha's brother, Rajiv.

Sridhar fished out a mini camera he was carrying and wrapped its strap around his right palm as we headed toward Dr. Mehra's clinic. Mamatha led the way carrying the baby, and I followed her, carrying the baby's essentials in a basket.

I glanced at my watch. It was 11 a.m., precisely twenty-four hours since I had entered the hospital the previous day. A sudden and humbling realization dawned on me, annihilating the first of the many veils of shallowness that had clouded my psyche during my sheltered life.

The gift of sight.

It was the first of the countless blessings I had always taken for granted.

The stairway leading to Prabha Eye Clinic had been transformed into a seating area by patients and their companions. We carefully navigated through the gaps to the waiting room, which was just as packed. Elderly patients with dark glasses and crying infants with tightly taped eye bandages heightened my anxiety. A wave of gnawing fear of the unknown and impending doom washed over me. I gathered my thoughts and consoled myself internally, thinking, *It won't be all that bad.*

We waited for a while, and soon, a nurse emerged to rescue us and lead us into Dr. Mehra's spacious office, adorned with numerous sophisticated instruments.

"Hello, Uncle," Mamatha said.

"Come in, Mamatha," Dr. Mehra replied with a broad smile. He was a short, stocky man in his fifties with thick hair graying at the temples. He wore a white coat and moved around the room deftly on a swivel chair. "Let us see the baby, shall we?" he said.

Mamatha took the baby and sat in front of him.

Dr. Mehra approached our child's face with a monocle in his right eye while Mamatha held the baby on her lap. He gently opened my daughter's eyelids to examine her eyes. Our baby cried in distress, but Dr. Mehra did not stop or relent.

After a couple of minutes, Dr. Mehra got up, wheeled his chair over to a table with an optical instrument featuring many lenses, and asked Mamatha to sit across from him with our baby on her lap. He put eye drops in both the baby's eyes and adjusted his seat opposite her. "She will throw a tantrum. Just hold her tight," he said, exposing us to the first of many examinations.

He started examining the baby's eyes with the instrument, using one hand to direct a blue light into the eyes and the other to look through the eyes with a magnifying lens and light to check the fundus (the inner portion of the eye visible through the pupil).

I sat on a chair in one corner, observing the procedure, while Sridhar stood next to the doctor, watching him intently.

Dr. Mehra peered into the fundoscopy for several minutes, then pulled back his swivel chair and addressed us. "It looks like a case of acute myopia with coloboma. It is very early to make a thorough diagnosis. We will wait for a few more weeks. Meanwhile, I will prescribe glasses that you should immediately put on her. We will have to wait a few weeks before deciding further steps."

"Is she able to see, Uncle?" Mamatha asked, her voice quivering.

He turned toward me to answer, as in India, there was a fear among doctors about the mental vulnerability of postnatal mothers. He did not want to tell Mamatha directly. "Normally, it is impossible to determine the visual development of newborns. She has some ocular anomalies, and we will have to wait and watch for a few weeks. But I don't think you should be too worried. Often, many ocular anomalies correct themselves in infants."

I looked toward Mamatha; she seemed relieved.

"What is myopia with coloboma?" I stuttered.

Dr. Mehra seemed a little annoyed by my questioning at this point, clearly not wanting to discuss more in front of Mamatha. "I can explain better to your brother. Can you, Mamatha, and the baby wait outside for a moment?" He removed his gloves and gestured us toward the door.

While Mamatha remained rooted in positive thinking and optimism, I sensed bad news. The fact he did not want to discuss his assessment with me or Mamatha but with Sridhar could only mean one thing—something was terribly wrong.

We decided to wait outside, as it was too full in the waiting room.

"What do you think?" Mamatha asked me once we found a bench to sit on.

I shrugged and turned away to conceal my reaction.

We waited for ten minutes before Sridhar joined us. When he did, he handed over Dr. Mehra's diagnosis, which he'd written in three illegible lines. I could read only three words: "Coloboma, Fundus Myopia."

"But what is this, Sri?" I asked.

"A coloboma is a defect in the iris of the eye, giving the pupil an irregular shape. Myopia is short-sightedness. She must wear glasses."

"A five-day-old baby?"

"Haven't you seen kids wearing glasses before?"

"Yes, Sri. But newborns?"

"Get the specs for the glasses and order them right away," Sridhar said.

"In a way, I'm relieved, Sri. The fact that Dr. Mehra advises spectacles must mean my daughter can see. Right?"

Walking next to me as we headed home, Sridhar remained silent. Only upon reaching Mamatha's parents' house did he say, "Mamatha, I'd like to have coffee with Mohan. Please tell your parents we'll be back soon."

She went into the house with our baby, then my brother and I went to a nearby café.

I watched Sridhar sipping his coffee. He was quiet and unsure of what to say. "Sri, does my baby have a serious problem?"

"Hey, don't jump to conclusions. It is too early to say anything conclusively," he said, deflecting my concern.

I was nervous but wanted him to be straightforward with me.

"It is too early to say anything, Mohan. Sometimes everything becomes okay as the baby grows."

"Myopia is short-sightedness. That is not a worry, right? But how serious is coloboma?" I strained my brain to understand more.

Sridhar paused and then looked at the floor. "I have to be honest with you, Mona." He took a deep breath, and I could see him make the decision in that moment to tell me what he was truly thinking. "There was no pupillary reaction in either of her eyes when I flashed my camera at her earlier during the exam."

It took me a couple of seconds to grasp the implication of his statement. I wondered why he had his camera. I'd read in novels about comas and pupillary reactions. The absence of a pupillary light reflex meant my child was unable to perceive light fully. She had either minimal or no vision. A wave of unbearable sadness and pity for my baby engulfed me, and I felt like breaking down. I pressed my lips together and swallowed my sorrow.

Sridhar looked at me and looked away when he saw my eyes getting moist. "Certain things that happen in life are just unfair, Mona. What can you do?"

My heart sank, for I knew my daughter was born blind, but Sridhar refused to say the "B" word aloud.

We returned to Mamatha's parents' house. Sridhar's car was waiting out front and he left for Mysore to be with his own newborn son. Mamatha was sitting on one of the sofas with our baby on her lap, and her mother sat next to her. My father-in-law was seated across from Mamatha.

"Mohan, there is no need to say anything about the baby's problem to anyone," Ranga Swamy said, looking at me while his right hand squeezed the sofa armrest.

A feeling of shock and a sense of repulsion added to my already sad state.

Mamatha stared at me, studying my reaction.

I looked at my mother-in-law to gauge her take on all of this. With her face turned toward her husband, she glanced at me from the corner of her eyes. She appeared to agree with her husband. Neither of them wanted their relatives and friends to know their grandchild had a vision problem.

Did he want to keep it a secret because he was ashamed? As if it made him an inferior person, like hiding a scar behind a mask. Did he want to hide it because he did not want his relatives to indulge in speculations about the cause of our misfortune? My in-laws, as grandparents, were ashamed their grandchild was not "normal." Or was it guilt? Guilt for agreeing to the marriage alliance even though we belonged to the same *gotra*? (A lineage of people descended from an unbroken male line of a common male ancestor from thousands of years ago.) I could not tell. But I felt outraged. This day was the beginning of my and Mamatha's journey of societal persecution.

Mamatha started to weep but quickly gathered herself. Wiping her tears with her sleeve, she said, "Don't worry, Mohan, I will surely give you a healthy child."

"Come on, Mamatha, she *is* a beautiful and healthy child. I am sure she will be one hundred percent fine in time," I said, trying to convince both of us.

I spent the rest of the day sitting right next to Mamatha and my baby, each of us with so much to say to the other yet lacking the drive and fortitude to express it.

That evening, my production manager at Arvee, K.M. Srinivas, visited us in Bangalore to see my daughter, who was sleeping in the cradle. "Such a beautiful girl. Congratulations, sir," he boasted.

"Thanks," I mumbled.

As I ushered him out, he said, "Sir, our first batch of tetramisole will come out the day after tomorrow. Should we wait for your arrival before removing the material from the tray dryer?"

"Yes," I said, forcing my mind to shift from thoughts of my child.

My new company, Arvee Chem Pharma Pvt. Ltd., was about to become the first and only company in India to manufacture this pharmaceutical drug in bulk. As a leader, it was important I be present to compliment and congratulate the team. I had incorporated Arvee two years earlier to manufacture tetramisole, which is used for the treatment of parasitic worm infections in the intestine.

Mamatha must have overheard the conversation because as soon as I closed the door behind Srinivas, she asked, "Mohan, how long will you be here with me? You have companies to manage. They are new and need your presence."

Her sensitivity, thinking about my entrepreneurial obligations, comforted me, as I had presumed her worries would consume her.

Mamatha put up a bold front. She surprised me with her ability to rebound so quickly.

"I will go tomorrow and return as soon as possible," I said, a sliver of enthusiasm and celebration in my voice.

I reluctantly left for Mysore the following morning, traveling by taxi to see and applaud the team for the first commercial batch of our new product. All the major pharmaceutical companies in India were importing the drug at three times our selling price. The new manufacturing facility in Mysore, which I had personally supervised, had been completed in nine months. The plant had the capacity to produce 1,000 kilograms a month, with a manufacturing cost of 500 rupees per kilogram and a selling price of 950 rupees per kilogram.

I drove straight to the factory, and the excitement of seeing the finished product of the very first batch temporarily clouded my underlying sadness about our daughter's condition.

"Hello, Man," said Dr. Vaidhyanathan, greeting me in his usual style as he followed me to the finished product room.

The pure white powder was a treat to my eyes. With that, India produced its own commercial tetramisole for the first time. I felt a momentary pride, the success of my enterprise pushing aside the sadness of the recent shock. My new business had landed on the Indian pharmaceutical map.

Our first customer from the town of Baroda, who had been waiting for almost a week, picked up the entire batch and rushed back to his facility in Gujarat. I wanted to share the good news with

Mamatha, but the only way to contact her was through her parents' neighbor's phone, so I called them, and they got Mamatha on the line.

"Our first batch of tetramisole is a success!" I boasted.

"Congrats, Mohan. I am so happy for you!"

"How is our baby?" I asked.

"She's fine. I haven't been able to go get her glasses yet, though. Maybe on Monday?"

I struggled to stay optimistic; my thoughts jumped between two worlds. The sorrow stemming from my baby's potential eye condition abruptly overshadowed the momentary elation of my triumph in the commercial world.

Desperately seeking to distract my troubled mind from the shadows of my child's predicament, I longed to resurrect the carefree spirit of the old Mohan. On my way back to our Gokulam home, I bought a bottle of Old Monk rum from a local shop.

Arriving late in the evening, I immersed myself in Kitarō's evocative Japanese melodies on the CD player, severed ties with the outside world by disconnecting the phone, and stretched out on the sofa. I poured myself generous measures from the bottle and indulged in contemplative brooding. Feeling a bit cheerful after a few drinks, I polished off nearly three-quarters of the bottle over the next several hours, transitioning to my favorite Billboard hits of the '80s, forcing myself to celebrate and enjoy my business success. By around 2:30 a.m., my mind was thoroughly exhausted, and I fell asleep.

When I opened my eyes, it felt like a heavy rod had struck my head with full force. It was around noon the next day. The jolt was a hangover combined with the mental image of my baby's closed eyes. I felt extremely nauseous and ran to the bathroom. Kneeling, I gripped the commode with both hands, throwing up horribly and repeatedly. I felt sad and confused. The thought of a cruel deity mocking the turmoil of mere mortals like me burned me with wrath. My thoughts raced with a whirlwind of emotions: shock, self-pity, helplessness, anger, and profound sorrow. I now seemed to live in a world with a future gone dark. Never in my thirty-one years had I encountered such overwhelming grief. Tears cascaded down my cheeks uncontrollably. I was shattered.

What is in store for my daughter? How am I going to handle the situation? What will my future look like? How can I instill positivity and confidence in Mamatha? What will our lives be like from now on? We had been married for just over a year. Mamatha, only twenty-one and having been raised in a sheltered nuclear family, was unaccustomed to the harsh realities of life.

Why is all this misery happening to me? What have I done to deserve this? Could I have done something differently that might have changed the events of the past few days? I clung to the guilt, wondering if there was something I did that, if avoided, might have altered the outcome. I questioned and speculated endlessly, grappling with the age-old, fruitless query.

Why me?

Out of all the people in the world, and particularly among my parents' nine children, why was I chosen to bear a blind child? Was I a bad person, and was that why my daughter was born with a defect in her eyes? Was this tragedy due to some malevolent force?

Like a broken record, my mind replayed these questions in an endless loop, the answers forever out of reach.

Is it because I agreed to the forceps delivery? Is it revenge for a stray dog bite that required seven stitches around my navel when I was nine? Ever since then, I had pelted stones at stray dogs and was cruel to disobedient pets.

Is it because of the medication Mamatha took for the threatened miscarriage when she was four months pregnant? Have I unknowingly mistreated any blind person? I had never even met a blind person in my life.

Or was it because I was arrogant and disobedient to my elder brothers? Was this punishment divine retribution for confronting my brothers over my rights to our company?

Damn you, God!

With my head pounding from the hangover, I plugged in the phone and called my other brother whose wife's niece was severely autistic. "Did Sridhar tell you about my child?" I asked him, my voice heavy.

"Yes. Sridhar told me she has some issues with her eyes and has difficulty seeing. Don't worry. Everything will be fine," he said.

"Krishna, why do you think this happened to me, out of all seven brothers?"

He paused for a few seconds before delivering words that would scar me for life. "I think it is because of your arrogance, Mona."

I felt like an arrow had pierced my throat, leaving me speechless as I hung up the phone. I was now convinced what had happened to me resulted from malicious evil eyes celebrating that *life had shown me my place*. A grim conviction solidified within me: I deserved this divine retribution.

Suddenly, I was furious with myself, thinking of Mamatha alone with the baby. Overwhelmed with rage at myself and our fate, I took two paracetamol tablets, packed my bags, and left for Bangalore to be with Mamatha and our child.

I vowed never to drink again. Although I was not an alcoholic, a strong intuition urged me to give it up completely. I feared drinking might become an escapist coping mechanism. I made a conscious decision to face life's challenges head-on, committed to navigating this path with Mamatha by my side.

That was the first of 6,570 days of my complete sobriety.

Chapter 5

A World Out of Focus

(June 25, 1989 - January 1990)

It was late afternoon when I returned to my in-laws' house. The two paracetamol pills I took for the hangover had helped me drive non-stop to Bangalore through a rainstorm.

Water was dripping from several spots in the ceiling of the living room when I entered and I was now certain that God had decided to rain only on me. "The limestone waterproofing has come off," my father-in-law announced as I removed my shoes.

Mamatha's mother was busy placing plastic buckets and a few large cooking vessels under each seepage to avoid waterlogging. Luckily, the room where Mamatha and our newborn were staying had no such leaking. I went straight to their room, gave Mamatha a kiss hello, and noticed our daughter asleep in her crib. "Where is the Prabha Eye Clinic prescription?" I asked, noticing the time.

"It is next to Lord Krishna's portrait in the kitchen."

"I'll be back in a jiffy," I declared. Then I went to the kitchen, grabbed the folded slip, and left for the eye clinic to get spectacles for our baby.

The optometrist had a separate shop a little distance away from the clinic. He gave me a synthetic leather pouch measuring about three inches long and an inch wide. I opened it to see the tiny spectacle frame with large, thick lenses. I had never seen such a small pair of glasses in my life. My heart sank. It was a strange and surreal sight. Another painful, sorrow-filled choke automatically rushed to my throat, but I managed to console myself; *my child might be able to respond to my stuck-out tongue with the help of these spectacles.*

With glasses in hand, I returned to my in-laws' home and quietly entered the room where Mamatha was now resting. Our baby was still sleeping in the cradle. I sat next to Mamatha, took out the tiny empty leather pouch from my top pocket, and placed it on the table by the bed.

We were both noticeably tired, so I lay down beside my wife, and we drifted off with our new angel asleep in the crib next to us, her tiny fists curled near her shoulders. But our rest was short-lived, interrupted by the soft sounds of fussing from the crib.

Mamatha got up to calm her while I closely observed. *Will my daughter be all right? Is her hearing okay?* I stood up next to the cradle and tried snapping my fingers again like before. I was ecstatic when she reacted to the noise I made. I smiled at Mamatha and said, "The baby can hear very well."

"Of course, Mona. We both already checked that."

Mamatha reached to unclasp the top of her maternity gown, then asked me to bring our baby to her on the bed. The cradle was a metal family heirloom that even Mamatha had slept in as a baby. It had rusty, sharp edges and I would need to be careful while taking our delicate darling out of it—who was awake and calm now—so I motioned for Mamatha to bring the glasses over from the bedside table instead of feeding her right away. Tears began to roll down Mamatha's cheeks as she placed the glasses on our baby's tiny face.

"She's going to be fine, Mamatha. Her eyes will be okay, don't worry. This will help," I said in my most convincing voice.

But Mamatha could no longer hold back her sorrow and broke down inconsolably.

I was putting my arm around her when her mother came running inside. She saw her new granddaughter wearing glasses and softly said, "Take heart, Mamatha. The glasses are for her good. She will now start seeing well."

I anxiously gazed at my daughter for any change in her ocular movement. There was none.

"Her eyes look normal from the outside, don't they?" Mamatha asked between sobs.

"Yes, of course," I replied.

"Then why doesn't she look at us now that the glasses are on?"

"She's only a week old. I think her eyes need to develop more fully," I said, suppressing my emotions. I picked up our baby and held her until Mamatha was ready to nurse.

It had stopped raining by late evening, and the streetlight was peeping through the living room window. The doorbell sparrow chirped, a sound that still to this day sends a shiver down my spine. Dr. Jayaprakash was at the door, two hours late. I was relieved he came and hopeful he might have further insights to share.

Jayee was a fair and hefty man in his late thirties. It was kind of him to come and show his support, but unfortunately, he didn't have any further information to offer us. Instead, the family tried to speak of other matters, and I found myself feeling sidelined and ignored.

My mother-in-law sat on a chair across from me by the wall, leaning forward, supporting herself with her two palms face down by her side. She was a kind lady with the mildest manners and a timid nature, but you could tell she was feeling the stress of our situation.

Jayee tried to break the tension by asking about her son, Rajiv, Mamatha's lone brother, who had enrolled himself for an engineering degree in electronics at Hassan University. "How is Rajiv? Does hostel life suit him?"

"We received his letter yesterday. He is doing okay," Leela replied.

Breaking the awkwardness, our baby started to fuss and then cry. Mamatha hurried out of the room to calm her, with my mother-in-law right behind, reassuring her, "Relax, Mamatha, crying is good for babies."

Jayee looked at his watch and, with a gesture that conveyed he had to leave, put on his shoes and headed out. I felt displeased by his escapism.

That night, I struggled to come to terms with my situation. This pain was unlike any I had ever experienced before, like a knife twisting in my heart. The pain I experienced when my parents died or when I felt betrayed by my older siblings was nothing compared to what I was now feeling. Every time the possibility of my child being blind crossed my mind, I was overwhelmed with sadness, unable to find any words of comfort or hope.

I stayed with Mamatha for the next few days. I was in a new and unfamiliar state of mind, as if I were living in a world out of focus. It felt like no one understood or appreciated my level of mental distress. I judged everyone I knew as "you can't even fathom" people. The fact that Mamatha's parents did not want to acknowledge our child had an issue made me extremely agitated and sad. Even though they realized their grandchild had a problem, they did not want to talk about it.

My in-laws were embarrassed by their relatives' innocent queries about the glasses on our child. Ranga Swamy had a lot of friends visiting him, and he would normally call them inside lovingly to chat. But now, he started talking to them while sitting in the front foyer to avoid them seeing the bespectacled baby. He found it challenging to handle the sympathy friends and relatives needlessly extended when they saw the glasses on our daughter.

When our child was three weeks old, my mother-in-law broached the subject of naming our baby. The naming ritual in Hinduism involves studying the horoscope, the birth chart of the baby, and, based on it, deciding on an appropriate and astrologically proper name. Mamatha and I had to choose a name that started with the letter "Y" since our baby belonged to Jyeshta Nakshatra. I had been named Rama Mohana, as per Hindu astrology, because I was born under the birth star Purvashada Nakshatra and had to have a name starting with the sound "Ra." It was ultimately reduced to Mohan.

Mamatha had already found several names a few days earlier based on her discussions with a Hindu priest through her father. It was then we decided on "Yogita" as our daughter's name. Yogita in Sanskrit means "to mesmerize or enchant."

The famous Devagiri Temple, of which my father-in-law was a founder trustee, deputed an expert priest for these rituals. He chose the morning of August 3rd to be the most auspicious date and time. Our child would be six weeks old by then. Customarily, close family, relatives, and friends would gather and shower their blessings of well-being and good health onto a new family member. In our case, there would be just six of us—Mamatha, her brother Rajiv, her parents, Yogita, and me.

The ritual started at 10 a.m. On a bronze plate, the pundit created a thick layer of rice grains. He asked me to write "Yogita" on the layer with a gold stick. He then asked me to whisper the name "Yogita" into our baby's right ear four times, along with a prayer, which I did with all my heart.

"It is with great joy that Mamatha and I accept from God the gift of our child. We present to you, our family and community, this our child, whom we call Yogita and today dedicate to God. May our child and her name be forever enrolled in the Book of Life."

It was a simple ritual by any standard. The red sweater with white stripes that Mamatha had lovingly knit for Yogita during her pregnancy looked impossibly small. But as soon as Mamatha placed it on her and fastened the buttons, Yogita looked angelic and cozy.

During the following days, Mamatha would hold Yogita on her lap and excitedly wave a bright blue and white rattler back and forth, waiting in eager anticipation for Yogita to follow its movement with her eyes. But to Mamatha's growing heartbreak, Yogita remained still and unresponsive to any visual stimuli, even while wearing the glasses.

With each passing day, Mamatha watched in agony as Yogita's blindness became more apparent.

As I watched this reluctant acceptance unfold, I resolved that Mamatha and Yogita would be my main priorities. I stopped socializing the way I used to.

When Yogita was three months old, Mamatha decided to return from her parents' house to our Gokulam home in Mysore, so in September, I brought them back from Bangalore. Mamatha's mother came with us to stay a week and help us settle in.

As I opened the front door of our Gokulam house, my new family following close behind, I realized the magnitude of my responsibility and the fact that my life, as I had lived it so far, was over. I was entering a completely new phase of existence. With this new awareness, I felt I needed to make significant changes. It had been a couple of months since I had stopped socializing and drinking. I felt the least a husband and father could do for the sake of his family was to be emotionally and physically available to them twenty-four-seven. Initially, it was a challenge. I still had new businesses to shepherd, but I was determined to change who and what I used to be. I avoided all my friends and relatives, isolated myself outside of work, and read books on babies and their development.

Penelope Leach's book *Your Baby and Child*[1] was one of the first books I devoured. I pored over every page, searching for information on vision and other developmental milestones. According to the book, a healthy baby's head should steady itself by three months; they should be able to follow objects by five or six months, crawl by six to nine months, and walk by their first birthday. I knew Yogita would be significantly behind for most of those milestones. I had to come to terms with my lack of control over life events and the world around me.

By November, Yogita could only turn her head completely and awkwardly toward her right side whenever she slept. She always looked down and only occasionally lifted her head. The back of her skull was flattened, with a protrusion on the rear left side, which made it difficult for her to turn her head to the left while sleeping. We tried stuffing a small pillow under the flattened side to straighten her head, but it didn't help. Her head would eventually slip back to the right side. Although her head slowly became steadier by the time she was five months old, she continued to always look down. The most challenging part was that there was no user manual for parents like us, who faced such a unique and daunting challenge. Whenever Mamatha cried, I tried to console her, though my voice was always heavy with emotional stress and defeat.

At one point, we tried to go to the new Krishna temple that had opened in our neighborhood, our first outing with Yogita. While there, we noticed another devotee who had brought his wife and their three-month-old son. The mother carried her baby on her shoulder, his little head turning almost 180 degrees as he looked around curiously. In contrast, I carried Yogita on my shoulder, her tiny hands clasped together, her gaze fixed downward.

Suddenly, Mamatha hurried back to the car, and I followed her. Through tears, she cried, "I can't bear to watch other babies, Mona. Did you notice that little baby? Look at poor Yogita!"

I couldn't say anything; I was choked up too.

Seeing other children Yogita's age experiencing the world with wonder was heartbreaking. For Mamatha, it brought waves of self-pity, while for me, it stirred up jealousy and anger. The disparity between Yogita and other infants her age was too much to bear.

After that, Mamatha and I began to withdraw from socializing altogether. It was excruciating to watch other children achieve the usual milestones. I desperately wanted people to understand, but conversations became awkward and strained. Friends and relatives didn't know what to say, and their inability to relate made me feel alone. Mamatha found a way to stay positive, but I felt no one could truly comprehend or appreciate our emotional burden.

Despite the outward challenges, I would marvel at how Mamatha embraced all the basics of mothering an infant. What fascinated me most was the way she mastered the art of bathing our baby, Indian style. Mamatha would keep Yogita on her outstretched legs, with the baby facing downward, ensuring she wouldn't slip or fall. After massaging Yogita's entire body with sesame oil for fifteen minutes, she followed up with a warm water bath using a mug, maintaining a consistent routine. She bathed Yogita twice a week.

During these early days, I began to appreciate the gift of family. My brother, Krishna, was right—I had been arrogant. I used to love myself more than anyone else in the world. My attitude was always, *I love you, but I love me more. I have needs, too; sorry.* But now, I was learning that my needs were less important than my family's. I was coming to love my family more than myself. And yet, I still struggled. I felt guilty and afraid of enjoying even the simplest pleasures, fearing that more tragedies might befall us. I felt guilty for laughing too hard, as if, under the circumstances, it was inappropriate. Deep down, I believed in my sadness and trusted my fears because I felt I had received what I deserved for some past sinful behavior.

I lost sleep over what some family members were saying about our lineage, that Brahmin couples who marry within the same gotra will perish. Though Mamatha and I belonged to the same gotra, the original progenitor lived thousands of years ago. It was like saying all Christians are related since they all hail from one couple, Adam and Eve. Despite these troubling superstitions, Mamatha remained focused on upholding other, more meaningful traditions that guided our way of life.

One such tradition was ear lobe piercing, known as *Karnvedh Sanskar,* which had to be performed on Yogita. It is considered a significant ceremony among Hindus in many traditions—one of the sixteen major rites a Hindu must undergo in life.

Typically performed during the sixth or seventh month, it is believed ear piercing helps maintain hormonal balance in girls as they grow older and aids in the flow of energy throughout the body. A goldsmith or a doctor can carry out the ceremony. A goldsmith uses gold needles, as gold never rusts, to pierce the earlobe, while doctors perform the procedure with a sterilized needle.

Mamatha was eager to have Yogita's ear lobes pierced before she turned seven months old, but the thought of making Yogita cry brought a lump to my throat. We decided to go to a doctor and visited a clinic near our house run by a female physician. Thankfully, the gun piercing caused Yogita to sob only mildly for a few minutes, sparing Mamatha her precious tears and me my melancholy. We needed to insert gold rings in her earlobes, so we went to Komal Jewelers nearby to buy earrings for Yogita.

While Mamatha browsed the myriad of earrings on display beneath the glass, I gazed at the diamond jewelry behind the cash counter. An older man, around sixty, who seemed to be the shop owner, stood behind the counter. He kept staring at Yogita, who was playing with her fingers, her eyes closed.

"Your daughter?" His voice held a note of sympathy, and his following words were the shallowest consolation I had ever heard.

"My granddaughter has Down syndrome," he said as he placed the earrings in a box. "I'm happy because she's saved us millions in dowry and gold that we Marwaris would otherwise have to shell out if she were normal, and we had to marry her off!" He grinned.

My repulsion at his words nearly made me ask if he was willing to donate his eyes for a few million bucks, but I held back. Was money truly a consolation to his grandchild's good health? Or perhaps this was his way of coping, justifying his own injustice. Who was I to judge his priorities? But to me, equating and justifying a child's disability with money saved on wedding expenses was not just inhumane; it was simply wrong. As Robert Hensel, the wheelchair champion, rightly pointed out, *"There is no greater disability in society, than the inability to see a person as more."*[2]

As I glanced at Mamatha, I was relieved the jeweler's words had not registered with her. I drove home in deep thought, reflecting on the naive and pristinely innocent Mamatha I had met just two years before. I couldn't help but envy all those parents whose children were healthy. The overwhelming sense of inadequacy was all-consuming, and I felt justified in my bitterness as if it were a natural response to the situation.

In my darkest moments, I wished all the children of the world had been born blind so their parents would grieve just as I did.

CHAPTER 6

Blind-Sided

(September 1989 - January 1990)

Within a few months of commencing commercial production of tetramisole, my pharmaceutical venture, Arvee Chem Pharma, suddenly began facing unexpected challenges. Our customer from Baroda, who had camped in Mysore to pick up the first 60 kg batch just after Yogita was born, began to cancel his remaining orders for the rest of the year. Within days, every prospective customer called to cancel their orders as well.

The largest customer of tetramisole in India was Ambika Tarabai. I rushed to Mumbai (then known as Bombay) to speak with their purchasing manager, Vikram, to find out what was going on.

Vikram leaned back in his leather chair, tapping his fingers on the desk. His expensive Rolex appeared larger than his wrist. "The market for tetramisole is volatile right now," he said without a hint of concern. "Tetramisole has been available since last week at 400 rupees per kilogram. Chinese manufacturers are dumping container loads of tetramisole into the Indian market through Hong Kong."

"This is less than our raw material cost," I replied in disbelief.

"How could you not know?" he asked.

As if I don't have enough on my plate already, I thought, feeling an instant surge of anger and persecution. There was no point in burdening him with my personal woes. "I've got a lot going on," I mumbled.

We had produced slightly more than 1800 kgs in three months, and customers had only picked up about 900 kgs. With nearly 1,000 kgs lying unsold, we needed more money to procure additional raw materials. I needed to liquidate the stock somehow.

I called Dr. Vaidhyanathan, my technical director and business partner, right then and there from Vikram's office. He consoled me by emphasizing that our tetramisole was far superior in terms of purity and assured me that all the Indian customers would return to us within weeks. However, as I met with other distributors in Mumbai that day, many of them disagreed about the purity of the Chinese material.

"Mohan, all I have to do is give the Chinese product a solvent wash. I may lose five percent of the material and spend a little on the solvent, but even then, my cost will be less than half of your price," said the purchase manager of a large US-based pharmaceutical company. Although the Chinese tetramisole was brown and clumped up due to improper crystallization and drying, they still saw it as a better deal.

I had at least six meetings with various customers and distributors by midafternoon. These companies were the same ones that had encouraged me during my market survey to provide my product to them. But now, they were unwilling to pay extra for Indian material just because we made it in India.

I decided that day to hire my own distributor and marketing agent who specialized in bulk pharmaceuticals. There were dozens of them on Princess Street in Mumbai. Gautam Gandhi impressed me the most out of the several agents I met the following day. He was a couple of years older than me, well-educated, and appeared reliable and honest. His firm, Chem-Pharma, specialized in importing specialty chemicals and APIs from China, and in his tastefully decorated office, he sat behind a large wooden desk with several phones. Like Vikram, he was dressed expensively, wearing designer jeans and gold-plated glasses.

I confessed my helplessness openly to Gautam. "I have no idea what to do next, Gautam. Please help me."

"I feel sorry for you, Mohan. Let me see what I can do."

"But what do I do with my unused 1,000 kgs of tetramisole?"

"You can do one thing. Appoint me as a consignment sales agent on a commission basis and send your inventory to me. It won't be too difficult to sell 10 to 20 kg lots at a 30 percent discount to small consumers and clear your inventory."

"I can't afford to pay any fixed monthly expenses," I replied.

"That's okay. Just pay me a five percent commission on whatever I sell," Gautam said, much to my relief.

Back in Mysore, we immediately dispatched the 1,000 kgs to Mumbai.

As for the future of manufacturing tetramisole, I could think of only one solution: persuade the Ministry of Commerce and Industry to either ban the import of tetramisole or impose a hefty anti-dumping duty. At the time, the Indian government was focused on import substitution and encouraging local industries to reduce the country's dependence on imports.

One of my father-in-law's friends and neighbors, B.K. Chandrashekar, was a politician. Ranga Swamy offered to take me to him to explore the possibility of speaking with influential policy-makers in New Delhi. So, Mamatha, Yogita, and I drove to see our in-laws for a visit. I would meet with B.K. Chandrashekar, who lived right next door.

My father-in-law and I appeared at B.K. Chandrashekar's door.

"Welcome, Mr. Ranga Swamy," said the scholarly-looking Chandrashekar, dressed in white.

My father-in-law introduced me and explained why I was there.

Turning to me, Chandrashekar said, "It's commendable that you're the only manufacturer in India to have developed an important, commercially available pharmaceutical drug."

"Thank you, sir."

"How old are you?"

"I'm thirty-one."

"I will write a note to my friend, Ramakrishna Hegde, now a cabinet minister in charge of planning in the central government. I'm sure he will help you."

Chandrashekar wrote the letter to his friend and then handed it to me.

Two days later, I flew to Delhi from Bangalore to meet with Ramakrishna Hegde. At 11 a.m., I arrived at our government building, Yojana Bhavan, and entered his office.

"Do you have an appointment?" his secretary asked, glancing at my business card and Chandrashekar's letter.

"No," I replied.

"You'll have to wait. He's in an important meeting."

I nodded and settled into one of the stiff chairs in the waiting area, clutching my briefcase. The room buzzed with activity—telephones ringing, hushed conversations, the rhythmic clack of typewriter keys. Occasionally, the secretary's voice cut through the air as she answered calls with polished efficiency.

At first, I tried to distract myself by skimming through a stack of outdated magazines on the nearby table. The headlines were old news, the glossy pages worn thin by countless hands. I flipped through them absently, but the words refused to register. My mind kept circling back to the stakes of this meeting, with the fragile hope tied to that letter.

Finally, around 5 p.m., the secretary looked up from her desk and walked toward me, her expression a mix of impatience and professionalism. "He's ready to see you now," she said curtly. "You have ten minutes."

I exhaled, tension loosening its grip on my shoulders. Gathering my things, I straightened my tie and stepped forward, ready to make my case. Six hours of waiting had tested my patience; it had also steeled my determination.

I entered Mr. Hegde's office, which was larger than my entire house. It was intimidating. Mr. Hegde looked every bit the statesman and icon he was reputed to be. His dark Nehru coat stood in striking contrast to his white beard.

Thankfully, being very sharp, he quickly grasped my situation and instructed his secretary to contact the ministry to investigate my case, then prepare a note for me to bring to the ministry the following day.

Once at the ministry, they instructed me to meet with Mr. Kutino, a bureaucrat and undersecretary to the commerce minister. Being able to see him so quickly, I thought I had just won the battle. Unfortunately, I couldn't have been more wrong.

"Why should the government deprive its citizens of cheaper medicines by banning Chinese imports just to protect Indian companies? Find a way to make your drug cheaper than the Chinese companies," the secretary said with no hesitation or concern for my problem.

"But Chinese companies have sector-wise export targets that are fully subsidized by the government. Moreover, Chinese exports are more about political strategy and long-term global domination than about immediate commercial gains," I countered.

"I don't believe that. Anyway, leave your appeal letter with me, and I'll see what I can do." He stood up and offered his hand, signaling the conversation was over.

"Sir, doesn't import substitution play a key role in the new government's economic policy?" I asked.

"Yes, but we're talking about medicines here, not cosmetics," he said with a tone of indifference, then continued. "Look, you're here discussing problems that run into millions of rupees, whereas the smallest figure the ministry considers is in the billions. Before they set the next import-export policy, why don't you approach the commerce ministry through your chamber of commerce and your Director of Small-Scale Industries? They might consider your case. You never know."

That would be a year away, which felt like a lifetime to me.

Since Yogita was born, my business life seemed to mirror my personal life. I felt lost and inexperienced handling such matters, running from pillar to post. I knew little about how things worked in the power corridors of Delhi. No one seemed to care about my problems. Being new to the industry, I was frustrated, with no idea who to turn to or where to go. Fortunately, I was made of sterner stuff and refused to crumble under the assault of adversity. My saving grace was the share of assets I had received from the joint family kitty, allowing me to survive for a few more months.

I booked the next plane back to Bangalore to be with Mamatha and Yogita for a few days.

The flight was delayed by five hours due to early morning fog in New Delhi. As I sat alone at the Delhi Airport departure gate, I looked out through the large glass windows at an aircraft landing smoothly, and my thoughts began to wander. *What would happen if it suddenly crashed?* I shook my head in self-ridicule for having that thought!

I glanced up at the cloudy sky, hoping providence might take pity and bail me out of the double whammy of both personal and business upheavals. I sighed, watching a cloud that resembled the contour of a buffalo.

Why is God playing such cruel games with me? My thoughts persisted. Perhaps this was a karmic payback for my past behaviors?

My mind went back to my father, N. Ranga Rao, who founded our family business, N. Ranga Rao & Sons, in 1949. In keeping with the gender norms of the mid-20th century, the company name excluded his daughters from joining. Through relentless effort, he grew the business into a profitable and thriving enterprise within a decade. My father's work ethic was unwavering—he often cycled for miles, tirelessly selling his products and ensuring steady growth for the company.

Seven years after our father died, on a Tuesday morning in August 1987, I sat with my six elder brothers for our weekly family business meeting. In only four years, I had built a successful range of instant food products and launched a new pharmaceutical project. Leaning back, I frowned at the over-steamed *idlis* in front of me.

"Just shut up and eat, Mona. We all know you're the food expert now," Venkatesh joked.

I dangled an idli and remarked, "I can't understand how you guys tolerate this. I'll have dosas at Idli Mane later."

Venkatesh swatted at me, but I ducked just in time.

The clinking of spoons and the hum of the ceiling fan created a relaxed, familiar atmosphere. Outside the room, the sounds of lunch boxes being packed and kids running around blended with the chatter of our five sisters-in-law.

For the past two years, these Tuesday breakfast meetings had been a tradition. Held at our large family home, Sita Vilas, we used these sessions to address business and personal matters. After breakfast, Murthy pulled a slip from his shirt pocket, carefully unfolded it, and laid it on the table as if revealing a hand of cards.

"Nobody's getting any younger. It's time we clarify our roles in the business," he said, sliding the paper toward Guru, who examined it and passed it along silently. We all studied the proposal. It outlined new roles, changes in leadership, and a division of ownership. Sridhar and I would no longer be partners in the family firm.

I was more shocked by the suddenness and casual nature of such a monumental decision than by the proposal itself. The audacious plan Murthy had laid out would split up a 150-million-rupee business built by my father over forty years ago.

While Murthy had long complained about clarifying roles and leadership accountability, a change in ownership and my removal was unimaginable. Our mother had just passed a few weeks prior, in June 1987, and now Murthy was proposing to split what we had shared equally, leaving the first three brothers with the cream and the rest of us with the skimmed milk—a reality they staunchly denied.

"As per your proposal, Sridhar and I will no longer be partners in the family firms?" I asked.

Murthy seemed shaken, not by the content, but by the act of questioning itself. He had expected unconditional obedience, especially from me, the youngest.

"You have new businesses you're interested in. We'll take care of your financial security. What's your problem?" Murthy shot back, dodging my question.

"Shouldn't experienced members help build new businesses while newcomers learn from the established ones?" I asked, feeling entitled.

Murthy's face turned red. "You're not listening. This firm is what it is because of me. I can't keep working without knowing my future role."

"If Sridhar and I had started earlier, giving up our studies, would we be equal contributors?" I countered.

Clearly feeling attacked, Vasu cut in angrily, "Watch what you say."

Guru then surprised me: "Leave Sridhar to me. Speak for yourself."

I raised my voice. "I've been here for four years. How can you say I haven't contributed? I've risked a lot starting two new companies."

"You're not a risk-taker. You're a gambler," Murthy retorted.

Guru intervened. "Relax."

But the damage was done. Silence fell, broken only by the sound of raindrops outside.

Deep down, I had always feared I wasn't enough and didn't deserve a share in my father's business. Nevertheless, I earned an M.B.A. and began learning the ropes in our businesses. I felt betrayed. Murthy had pushed me out for no fault of my own. It was not fair.

Angrily, I stormed out of Sita Vilas, deciding never to be where I wasn't wanted. Though my new businesses were still in their infancy, I resolved to never let anyone take advantage of me again.

My life will be a one-man show, I swore to myself.

Guru and Murthy unfolded a proposal that reshaped the future of our family businesses and irreversibly scarred our brotherly bond. Whether my brothers felt I threatened their lifestyles and their children's futures, or they had been waiting all along for my mother to pass away to usurp the consistently profitable business, I don't know. Murthy became harsh, demanding partition. His proposal, which eventually escalated into a full-blown war, sought to restructure the ownership of the main family firm that generated over 80 percent of the revenues and profits. The eldest three brothers would be the only partners, while Krishna and Venkatesh would jointly own smaller subsidiaries of the core family incense business. They would exclude me from all the family firms.

The revelation of my unwantedness shattered my illusion of security and trust. Their rejection reinforced a deeply hidden fear that had haunted me since childhood—the fear of being unwanted. This complex feeling was rooted in my early years as my parents, busy managing the family business, brought me to live with my two eldest brothers when I was two years old. My brothers were my heroes, my guardians, and my foster parents, and although I always felt loved, my parents did give me over to them for my formative years.

After being usurped, I could no longer see my brothers as the childhood idols I once admired; they now appeared uncaring, as intolerant adversaries. I fought for my rights, pointing out it was my father who had started the firm and made me an equal partner and that they had no right to reverse this position after his death. They met my resistance with claims that I had disregarded the contributions of the eldest brothers. Realizing the futility of my anger, I decided to step away from them and carve out a place in business I could call my own.

Now, two years later, I felt guilty and morally afraid that my transgressions were the root cause of my suffering. All of my nephews and nieces were born without any anomalies, while my child was born blind. I still had not found an answer to the soul-burning question: *Why me?* I was now convinced that what was happening to me was divine retribution for my past wrongs.

Suddenly, I was jolted by the blaring announcement for the commencement of boarding.

When I returned to my Arvee office in Mysore, I faced the urgent need to come up with funds for salaries and wages. Even the bank interest was overdue, and I was in dire straits. Arvee had been without any work for more than six months. I had to inject funds for salaries and wages to keep the company afloat. I managed a team of fifty-eight, with Dr. Vaidhyanathan as the technical director and myself as the commercial director.

I hoped for cash inflow from the 1,000 kgs of tetramisole that I had entrusted to our consignment sales agent in Mumbai, worth almost a million rupees. Whenever I tried to reach Gautam, his office would inform me that he was away in Hong Kong or New Delhi.

Finally, after a fortnight, I got through to him using a different name. "Gautam, we haven't received any payment for the 1,000 kgs dispatched. Please send at least Rs. 3 lakhs urgently," I pleaded.

"I'm sorry, Mohan, but I haven't been able to sell even a single kilo," Gautam said nonchalantly.

"What? You were confident of liquidating the stocks in small lots."

"Your price is two and a half times that of the Chinese. No one wants to buy your product, even with a 50 percent discount."

Deeply disappointed, I replied, "Please return the entire consignment, Gautam."

"Sure," he said and hung up.

After a month, the consignment arrived with intact labels and unbroken seals. But to my horror, Ravishankar, our quality control manager, came running to my office, screaming, "Sir, we have been cheated!"

What lay within those containers was not tetramisole HCl, our product, but a shocking revelation—every one of the forty drums, each holding 25 kgs, contained worthless white chalk powder that matched the appearance of tetramisole.

I sent my manager to Mumbai with a sample of the consignment to confront Gautam and have him call me immediately.

"What the hell, Gautam! The consignment you sent contains chalk powder, not tetramisole HCl!" I yelled at the top of my voice, only to be met with a chilling revelation.

Gautam's words, uttered with a sinister calmness, cut through the air like a blade. "I just sent back whatever you had dispatched to me. Your inventory has been lying untouched. What your manager has brought with him is what I received. In fact, I didn't even see your consignment," he lied, his words resonating with the echoes of a betrayal so meticulously orchestrated.

I called my lawyer at once, who told me there was nothing I could do against Gautam. If I had to pursue legal action, I could only sue the transporter, TRL, a massive corporation.

The revelation hit like a thunderbolt, reinforcing my belief it was divine retribution ensnaring me for my sins rather than what it was: an intricate web of deceit.

This betrayal felt like a recurring pattern now. I felt blind-sided once again—first by my brothers, then by my daughter's health, and now my business. When providence decides to target you, everything can fall apart. Trust becomes a chink in your armor, and ill fortune, your constant companion.

From feeling like a superhero a year earlier, I now felt like an eel at the bottom of the Indian Ocean. Once proud, overconfident, and dismissive, I had become timid, sad, and lost. It was as though a secret deal had been struck between my fate and my destiny to teach me a lesson, to test my mettle.

I was not alone. Mamatha was with me, and I found solace in her presence. However, Mamatha was battling her own demons, feeling responsible for the baby's vision loss and carrying an emotional burden infinitely greater than mine.

We were united in our struggle against a common adversary—destiny.

CHAPTER 7

Eyes Wide Shut

(January - April 1990)

Our evenings at home would usually start with the soft cooing of Yogita, wide awake in her crib, eagerly reaching for her favorite toys and bringing them to her mouth. I'd finish my dinner, lift her from the crib, and place her on the bed. A few tickles on her feet would set off uncontrollable giggles, filling the room with joy despite our exhaustion.

Yogita's sleep patterns were reversed—awake through the night and sleeping during the day. Mamatha often begged me to stay up with her until midnight to give her some much-needed reprieve. I obliged as often as I could.

One particular evening, Mamatha came over to join in the tickle fun. "I want to call her Turry," she said, positioning herself to tickle Yogita's toes.

"Why Turry?" I asked.

"Because she mumbles 'tuuurrry' whenever we tickle her!" she replied, unable to contain her laughter as she proceeded to tickle her perfect little feet. "Tuku Duku Turry Purri. My favorite Churumuri," she continued, her laughter spilling out with genuine joy. *Churumuri*, a spicy puffed rice snack, was and still is one of Mamatha's favorites.

I stood there watching her, feeling a mix of amazement and admiration. Mamatha's world had always been full of warmth and affection, shaped by the love of her parents, grandparents, and her younger brother. Her upbringing, filled with nightly storytelling sessions and nurturing family bonds, had given her an unshakable sense of optimism and trust in life's inherent goodness. Despite the fatigue, Mamatha embodied a sense of home—grounded, hopeful, and deeply connected to the simple joys of life.

Yogita, now fondly nicknamed Turry, was a cheerful child. She could entertain herself for hours as long as she was well-fed and left to play with her rattle toys. She had a contagious laugh that echoed through the house, especially when we laughed alongside her. She loved listening to nursery rhymes, and after much training, she would sometimes try to clap along to "If You're Happy and You Know It." Thankfully, Yogita was healthy in every way, other than her vision and development. Unlike kids her age, she never caught a cold or the flu.

Despite these small joys, I still guarded myself from feeling truly happy. Guilt would immediately follow if I allowed myself even a moment of bliss. I believed happiness wasn't appropriate under the circumstances of Yogita's condition. I felt I deserved my sadness and that my fears were justified because, deep down, I thought I had brought this upon myself as punishment for my sins.

As a coping mechanism, or perhaps as a lingering trace of arrogance from my past self, I would occasionally get a sudden sense of self-importance—a delusion that a divine and extraordinary assignment had chosen me. Almost immediately, though, I would be overcome with conflicting guilt, a deep shame for using Yogita as a trophy in my mind.

As we struggled our way through the challenges of Yogita's condition, it was equally difficult to get the support and understanding we needed from the people around us. When Yogita was around seven months old, a close relative visited our home and excitedly shared the news of her daughter's engagement with the son of a wealthy celebrity.

She asked all my brothers to help organize a grand wedding. It was common for us brothers to contribute financially since my relatives were less fortunate. I gladly gave 25,000 rupees, even though I was in a financial mess, as she had always been kind to me.

The wedding date was set, but I never received an invitation. The father of the bride called me a few days later to thank me for my help. "With much difficulty, I managed to convince this distinguished family to accept a middle-class family like mine," he said. "I want to ensure nothing goes wrong at the wedding, or that anyone sees anything inappropriate. I need everyone's help."

It took me a few moments to grasp the full meaning of his statement. He did not want Yogita to be seen at the wedding.

He was a mild-mannered gentleman who spoke very softly, so I hoped I was mistaken, but when they visited my eldest sister and all six of my brothers to invite them personally to the wedding and did not come to visit me, I knew I was right.

At that point, rather than confirm the situation with them, I decided I had no interest in going to the wedding. I lost all respect for these relatives and never treated them with the same regard I had prior. While I chose to forgive them, I could never forget how they perceived Yogita. However, they did me an unexpected favor in their avoidance—they deepened my love and resolve for my daughter.

Our friends and family members simply did not know how to navigate our strange and unfamiliar situation. To make matters worse, it was as though Mamatha and I were emperors with invisible clothes—pretending everything was fine when it was clear to everyone else that things were not. I still maintained that Yogita would regain her vision and that, with our love, she would be whole and healed at some point.

With that dedication to Yogita, I was often amenable to any unsolicited advice we regularly received from just about everyone. There were a myriad of recommended remedies, including "Carry out this ritual," "Perform that yagna," "Consult this Swamiji," and "Visit this temple and offer silver eye shades to the deity." They were all offered in hopes of a miracle that would cure Yogita. Driven by desperation, I dutifully performed every suggested ritual, believing there was something that would help Yogita gain her eyesight.

Previously in my life, the closest I had ever come to exploring non-scientific methods for healing was when I had conjunctivitis at the age of seven. My mother had used a few drops of our maid Kariamma's breast milk in my irritated eyes, and the condition disappeared. How I wished for a similar miracle cure for Yogita.

On top of the advice we received, Mamatha and I also sought out soothsayers, astrologists, palmists, and clairvoyants in our quest for answers and solutions. Our sole desire was reassurance that one day, Yogita would be able to see. One notable figure we encountered was Ganesh Alva, whose version of a crystal ball was an ancient Vedic text written on palm leaves. Mamatha's grandmother had recommended Alva. He practiced in Bangalore, and we went to him seeking answers.

When we met him at his home, Alva looked every bit the part of a shaman and soothsayer. The large talisman hanging from a silver chain around his neck and his loose, impeccably styled silk turtleneck gave him a mystical appearance. His home had an ashram-like feel, centered around a small room with a wooden book holder supporting a bundle of palm leaves inscribed with Sanskrit. The prominent sandalwood and red mark on his forehead contrasted sharply with his fair complexion.

Before Yogita was born, I would never have believed I would one day find myself in front of a soothsayer, placing faith in magical thinking and miracles. But now, hopefulness, guilt, and the fear that I had committed some sin needing absolution swirled within me. I was prepared to do anything—anything in the world—that could offer a solution to Yogita's problems. I resented how society allowed one aspect of her—her lack of vision—to obscure the rest of her being. This mental myopia reduced Yogita to just one trait: a girl who couldn't see.

We sat cross-legged in front of Alva, who was also sitting with a large bundle of palm-leaf manuscripts tied together before him.

He briefly explained the process. "First, I will match your life to the leaf and then proceed with my prediction. I will ask you a series of questions about your birthplace, date of birth, and other details. Once we locate your individual palm leaf, I will help you find direction and answers concerning your life."

Mamatha and I listened intently.

When he completed his questioning, he turned through multiple leaves before selecting one. "You've come about your child, haven't you?" he asked, shocking Mamatha and piquing my curiosity.

He must have deduced it from Mamatha's clothes, her large thali, and our sad expressions. I quickly dismissed the thoughts, trying not to judge him.

"It's about her eyes," he continued.

Okay. Now I was a bit stunned. But again, I was quick to assume he'd spied on us.

We nodded.

"She has a nerve problem in the brain, according to the leaf," he said, without elaborating on our daughter's vision.

"Will she see?" Mamatha's voice trembled.

He gave no direct answer, only repeating that Yogita had a nerve problem.

"You inadvertently killed a baby snake in this life or a past life, which has caused Sarpa Dosha. You must absolve yourself from this curse," he declared.

We Hindus have deep reverence for nature and all living creatures. Some believe that killing snakes is a grave sin, one that invites the curse of the serpents.

My already heavy sense of guilt over what had happened to my child now grew exponentially. "Yes," I admitted meekly, "when I was constructing my pharmaceutical plant, the workers killed a couple of snakes."

"You see," Alva continued, "Vedic astrology foretells that slaying a serpent causes an aberration in your astrological birth chart. This is known as *Sarpa Dosha*, or *Naga Dosh*a. It refers to the influence of the serpent planets—Rahu and Ketu—on a person's chart. This dosha typically occurs when Rahu or Ketu are positioned in specific houses, particularly the 5th, 7th, or 9th."

"How do I absolve myself, Guruji?" I asked, my voice low.

"You must perform the *Sarpa Dosha Nivarana Yagya* at Kukke Subramanya, a temple sacred to the Snake Gods. The yagna is crucial, as it helps to overcome life's challenges and lessens the malefic effects of Rahu and Ketu."

"What exactly is the procedure?" I asked.

"It's a complex, four-day ceremony involving prayers, offerings, and rituals meant to seek liberation from these afflictions. The *Sarpa Dosha Nivarana Yagya* neutralizes the bad karma of *Sarpa Dosha*."

"Will my child be able to see?" I asked, sounding like a child myself, desperate for hope.

"Definitely. Do not worry."

So, with a heart full of fear and hope, I resolved to plead with the Almighty, begging forgiveness for having inadvertently killed a snake.

The pilgrimage to Kukke Subramanya was nestled deep in the forests of the Western Ghats, about a six-hour drive from Bangalore.

"Please take my father with you," Mamatha pleaded when I told her I planned to go alone.

I agreed, and Mamatha's father, Ranga Swamy, took leave from work to accompany me on the journey. Together, we left for Subramanya.

The *Sarpa Samskara* ritual was carried out under the guidance of an expert priest, with Ranga Swamy assisting me throughout. The four days were emotionally draining and physically taxing. I spent the entire time consumed by devotion, terrified of making a mistake that could further anger the Gods.

A sudden realization struck me on the final day, after completing the ritual. There was something deeply unsettling about the idea of a supreme being who would heal Yogita only if I performed the right ceremonies. What kind of God, I wondered, would deprive an innocent child of something as vital as her eyesight, only to relent if her father performed the correct rituals and praised Him in the proper manner?

Upon returning home, my faith in God continued to waver while Mamatha's belief only grew stronger. She became even more convinced that good things would happen if we persisted in appeasing the Gods. Her upbringing, conditioned by her parents to always remain hopeful, made her bolder and more optimistic than me. Mamatha's refusal to think or speak negatively played an essential role in balancing my pessimism and overthinking. She often shared what her grandfather used to say, that "Invisible negative entities are lurking around, waiting for us to speak something negative. The moment they hear a negative phrase, they gleefully snatch it up and rush off to make it come true."

The days and weeks following the ceremony, I slowly began to absorb some of Mamatha's positive energy. Her unwavering optimism influenced me to seek self-help, spirituality, and philosophy books to guide me on developing such mindsets. Authors like Guy Finley, Sri Aurobindo, Wayne Dyer, and others offered me fresh perspectives on navigating the changes in my life. Their writings became a source of guidance, helping me foster personal growth and inner strength.

Soon, I grew to love being alone on this quest for liberating knowledge. It wasn't that I no longer suffered from our situation; I still asked the same old questions: *Why me? Why Mamatha? What now?* I continued to feel hurt and betrayed by unseen forces, and I developed a strong compulsion within me to resist letting go of my sense of persecution. I wanted to hold on to that grief as if it were my fundamental right *not* to overcome it too quickly.

Perhaps my grief is a powerful catalyst to begin a spiritual awakening within me, tearing away superficial layers of my being. As strange as it may sound, I found grieving to be cathartic, a relief, even a form of self-celebration. Whichever way I looked at it, while I was not keen on ridding myself of it quickly, I was open to finding new ways of looking at our situation.

Over time, I started to see that perhaps the world was more myopic than I was, unable to see beyond Yogita's blindness. They were visionless in their inability to appreciate her whole being, choosing instead to define her by a single anomaly. If a "typical" child stared at Yogita, I would take the opportunity to educate them. Smiling warmly, I'd invite the child to come closer and feel Yogita's face and body, helping them understand.

In her essay, "Welcome to Holland," Emily Perl Kingsley[3] beautifully expresses the experiences parents can go through when their child is different. To paraphrase her analogy: Imagine planning a trip to a renowned botanical garden celebrated for its stunning trees, flowers, birds, and serene ponds. You buy a guidebook and eagerly anticipate the marvels ahead. Yet, unexpectedly, your plans shift, and you find yourself in an uncharted jungle—no trails, roads, guide, or suitable guidebook in sight. As you navigate this unfamiliar terrain, you stumble, sustain injuries, encounter strange creatures, and begin to plead for direction. Over time, however, it dawns on you that you've arrived somewhere different. Gradually, you appreciate this unexpected journey, realizing it holds more richness and wonder than you ever anticipated. Mamatha and I hadn't landed in a strange and sinister land, just an unfamiliar one we had yet to discover and appreciate.

Gradually, as the months passed, I no longer drifted through life with my eyes wide shut. I began awakening to deeper truths I had never considered, moving beyond the surface-level concerns that once consumed me. The work and pride I selflessly poured into my new family became my anchor, grounding me in the love we shared. I continued striving to take better care of myself, waking up early to jog, and establishing an exercise routine. I needed to be strong for my family. My sobriety brought improved memory and focus, allowing me to stop wallowing in self-pity and no longer view our challenges as immense tragedies.

I was discovering a new sense of purpose and clarity in my world. An understanding that life was not without its difficulties, but I could choose to *not* let them define me. I began to look forward, trusting that emotional and practical solutions would present themselves as long as I remained open to them. This newfound strength gave me the courage to continue seeking advice and support from others, as I still held out hope that Yogita would someday be able to see.

CHAPTER 8

Vision of Hope

(April - June 1990)

Among my small circle of friends, the tall, handsome Shivdev was the most understanding, sensible, and sensitive about Yogita and our situation. He was the CEO of Resource, the advertising agency he founded, which handled the advertising for my food products. Scholarly, intelligent, and deeply spiritual, Shivdev and I had grown very close over time. During one of our regular coffee meetings, our conversation drifted, as it often did, toward Yogita. I had grown accustomed to talking about her condition with a mix of hope and quiet resignation, but this day felt different.

As I discussed the medical possibilities for Yogita's future, Shivdev listened intently, his eyes softening as I spoke. After a pause, he leaned forward and mentioned something I had not yet considered.

"You know, Mohan," he began thoughtfully, "my elder brother is a leading lung specialist at the Mayo Clinic in the U.S. He holds a senior position close to the directors."

His words piqued my curiosity. Shivdev had never spoken much about his family before, but this revelation felt like a key turning in a lock I hadn't known existed.

He continued. "Mohan, why don't you take Yogita to the Mayo Clinic? If there's one place where medical miracles happen, it's there."

The idea seemed almost too big to grasp at that moment, but something inside me stirred. "I've taken her to the best doctors in India, and all they told me was to put glasses on her," I replied.

"Mohan, the Mayo Clinic is at the forefront of eye-care research. You know they call it the Mecca of Medicine, right? My brother will go out of his way to help you there."

"Thanks, Shivdev. I'll give it some serious thought."

It didn't take long for me to decide, as a father, the least I could do for Yogita was to get her examined at the best hospital in the world.

That evening, I went straight to Mamatha with the idea. "Shivdev thinks we need to take Yogita to the Mayo Clinic, where his brother works. It's the best medical facility in the world, and I think we should go as soon as possible," I said. "What do you think?"

"Yes, Mohan! Yes!" Mamatha replied, clearly excited.

I already had a ten-year multiple-entry visa for the U.S., issued in 1986, but Mamatha didn't have a passport.

After she applied for her passport, I organized a thirty-day trip for June 1990, just a month and a half away, when Yogita would be exactly a year old.

Mamatha got her passport easily, and we were all set to leave India. Through Dr. Murali, a forensic psychiatrist in Pittsburgh and a classmate of one of my brothers, I was able to arrange an appointment with Dr. Hohberger, a pediatric ophthalmologist at the Mayo Clinic in Rochester. We had forwarded all of Yogita's reports to him via international courier, as faxing was still a rarity in 1990 India.

On the 4th of June, we boarded a British Airways flight with an eight-hour layover at Heathrow, set to arrive at Chicago's O'Hare Airport early the following day.

"Sir, you have to make your child sit in her seat and fasten her seatbelt," the air hostess said in a crisp British accent.

"Give me a couple of minutes, please," I replied, placing Yogita in her seat. She immediately started to scream, feeling alienated and disconnected. I took her back, held her close, and fastened the seatbelt around both of us. She soon fell asleep. Once the flight took off, I gently placed her back in her seat and tried to fasten the seatbelt. Yogita woke up and resumed yelling, so I held her close again.

As soon as the flight reached cruising altitude, Mamatha gently lifted Yogita and placed her in the bassinet attached to the side of the wall near the toilet. Yogita slept peacefully, like an angel. Thank goodness.

We arrived in Chicago at 10 a.m., tired but relieved to be so close to our destination. However, that relief was short-lived. An immigration officer with a broad build and a firm expression called the three of us aside and asked us to follow him. He led us into a small office, motioned for us to sit, and said, "I'm afraid I can't let the child enter the U.S., as she doesn't have a visa endorsed on either of your passports. You two can enter, but not her." His tone was firm, though it carried a hint of sympathy.

My heart skipped a beat. My face flushed with fear as I struggled to process the enormity of what he was saying. "We've traveled 8,000 miles just for her sake, and she's only eleven months old!" I pleaded, my voice trembling with desperation.

The officer nodded slowly, his expression softening, but he remained resolute.

"She's not a year old yet and doesn't have her own passport. Please, help us," I begged.

"Wait here," the officer said, leaving us in a state of panic.

The next half hour stretched endlessly, each minute laden with uncertainty. My mind raced through all the worst-case scenarios, but finally the officer returned—this time with an older African American woman by his side. Her eyes fell on Yogita, first with a stern, assessing gaze, but then something shifted. A look of understanding and empathy softened her features. She studied us for a moment before nodding at the officer—a simple, silent gesture that conveyed far more than words. Without hesitation, the officer stamped a three-month visa onto Mamatha's passport for Yogita.

Relief washed over me. When we finally stepped outside, the cold Chicago wind hit us like a slap, shockingly brisk for June. We pulled our jackets tight around us, trying to shield Yogita from the biting chill as we made our way toward the taxi stand, grateful that at least this part of the journey had ended on a positive note.

We stayed overnight in Chicago before taking an American Airlines flight to St. Louis, where we caught a connecting flight which landed us in Rochester, Minnesota. As we entered the arrival hall, a man in his early forties walked toward us with a warm smile. His slightly curled upper lip and gray hair immediately reminded me of the famous Indian actor, Dev Anand.

He reached his hand out to me. "Hi, I'm Dr. Jai, Shivdev's brother. Welcome to America."

"Hello, Doctor," I said, shaking his hand. "I'm Mohan, this is Mamatha, and this," I added, gently stroking Yogita's hair, "is our daughter, Yogita."

Dr. Jai looked at Yogita with affection. "Shivdev told me about you all," he said softly. He helped us retrieve our bags without hesitation and even picked up the largest suitcase.

"Please, don't worry about it. It's easy to pull along," Mamatha protested.

But the kind doctor waved off her concerns and carried the bag anyway. He asked us to wait outside the terminal while he went to fetch his car. In no time, a sleek white BMW pulled up, and Dr. Jai loaded our luggage into the trunk before driving us to his home in a quiet, upscale suburban neighborhood.

When we arrived, his wife greeted us at the door. She was a petite Indian woman with short-cropped hair, wearing a blue skirt patterned with large purple flowers and a sleeveless top. As we smiled at her, expecting warmth, she returned only a dry, emotionless look.

"You'll have to excuse me," Dr. Jai said, sensing the awkwardness but unable to stay. "I need to get back to the hospital." He left us standing in his pristine living room with his unsmiling wife.

Mamatha settled on an expensive-looking sofa, holding Yogita on her lap for feeding. Mrs. Jaiprakash's expression suggested disgust as if a pile of filth had fallen on her couch. Realizing her mistake, Mamatha quickly moved to the floor with Yogita to feed her.

The room fell into an awkward silence. To break it, I asked, "How long have you been in the United States?"

"Eighteen years," Mrs. Jaiprakash replied flatly.

"You're from Bangalore, I assume?"

"Yes."

A girl, around twelve or thirteen, dashed down the stairs with a notebook, asking for help in an American accent that was difficult to understand. I noticed her trying to sneak glances at us.

"Go back upstairs. Don't you see we have visitors?" Mrs. Jaiprakash snapped.

Shortly after, Mrs. Jaiprakash grabbed her car keys, yelled up the stairs to her daughter that she was going to the store, then said to us, "Excuse me, I need to get some groceries. I'll be back soon."

Left alone, we waited in silence for about ten minutes before I decided to call a cab. Leaving a note, we departed with relief when the cab arrived. The driver helped us choose the Civic Inn, a decent motel downtown close to the Mayo Clinic.

It was just after noon once we settled into our room, and we hadn't eaten yet, so we ordered a pizza from Pizza Hut.

"Mohan, why was that lady so cold and indifferent? You said they were eager for us to stay with them," Mamatha asked, puzzled.

"I'm just as shocked, Mamatha. I don't know why she acted that way. Maybe she thought we were here to ask for financial help or something. I honestly don't understand."

"Is everyone here like her?" Mamatha asked innocently.

"Not everyone, Mamatha. She probably sees India as a third-world country and doesn't want anything that reminds her of her roots. To her, we might look like we're seeking charity or shelter from her husband," I explained. "It seems like she's the one with vision issues that need fixing," I quipped.

A couple of hours later, I called Shivdev's brother to confirm where we had gone. He expressed shock and disappointment over our decision to leave and check into a hotel.

"I wanted to stay closer to the hospital," I feigned.

That evening, we headed to a nearby Italian restaurant for dinner and ordered pasta. For Mamatha, it was her second foreign meal, which she didn't enjoy.

"I'm really missing Indian food," she said. This trip was Mamatha's first exposure to the Western world. Despite speaking English fluently, she felt shy interacting with Americans.

Her next culture shock came when a pretty, buxom waitress leaned in close while speaking to me, her enthusiasm unmistakable. It was not something Mamatha was exposed to at all in India. On the opposite side, Mamatha was charmed by the sensitivity and politeness of other Americans we met. Our first such encounter was in the Civic Inn elevator. I was holding Yogita while she babbled, "Didil-Didil." We looked over to see an older man who smiled warmly at her and gently pinched her cheek.

However, not all Americans were as courteous, as I discovered the following morning at the hotel restaurant. The typical aroma of coffee and pancakes greeted us, and we chose a table in the corner. As I placed the room key and breakfast coupons on the table—essential for a complimentary breakfast—I noticed I had only two coupons.

When I asked Mamatha if we needed a separate plate for Yogita, she nodded. "I need some porridge and yogurt for her."

I approached the restaurant manager. "Can I have another coupon for my daughter?"

"For your doctor?" she asked.

"No, for my daughter," I repeated.

"For your doctor?" she asked again, raising her eyebrows at the word "doctor." Only then did I realize she was mocking my accent. She kept repeating it, with a hint of derision each time.

We Indians tend to pronounce "daughter" with a noticeable emphasis on the "t," which can sometimes sound like "doctor" to unfamiliar ears. But it seemed absurd for her to repeat it so many times. Why should it matter to her whether it was for my daughter or my doctor? She could have just billed me for the extra plate.

Her attitude was agonizingly humiliating, slicing through my already wounded sense of self. I flushed with embarrassment as I paid for the extra meal. After our breakfast, I went to the front desk for help to call a taxi to the Mayo Clinic.

I was surprised how close the Mayo Clinic was to the Civic Inn—under a thousand yards away. The taxi ride took less than two minutes, dropping us in front of a sleek, ten-story building.

Rochester, Minnesota, was a small town, yet it boasted the number-one-rated healthcare center in the world. The clean, architecturally stunning structure filled me with a sense of confidence. It was a vision of hope. I was staring at the mecca of medicine.

We entered the lobby and approached the patient registration desk.

"Hi. I'm Mohan Ranga Rao. I am—"

Before I could finish, the young, attractive attendant nodded in recognition. "Yes, Dr. Prakash informed us. Welcome to Mayo Clinic," she said, casting a warm glance at Yogita. "There is a form you need to fill out." She handed me a pad with the form and added, "I know you don't have insurance coverage, so you'll need to make a pre-care deposit." Her expression softened with sympathy.

"No problem. How much is it?" I asked.

"$6,000," she replied.

"Do you accept traveler's checks?"

"No. And additional deposits may be necessary if hospitalization is required."

I only had $2,000 in cash, but I did have $7,000 in traveler's checks that I could convert to cash. "Okay," I replied.

"Follow me," she instructed, leading us to the waiting area with pink walls adorned with animal paintings. While Yogita could show no interest in the art or the stuffed animals and toys scattered about, she seemed calm and content in the cozy environment.

The ambiance at Mayo Clinic was more akin to a retreat than a treatment center. The staff members were exceptionally cordial—smiling, cheerful, and eager to assist, holding doors open, and every interaction began with, "How are you today?" The atmosphere was unhurried and accommodating as someone guided us through the labyrinth of buildings to our next appointment.

We received a large envelope with booklets and catalogs on special education for children with disabilities. After a short wait, another young lady approached us and asked us to follow her. We walked quite a distance before arriving at the ophthalmology section.

A man in his early forties, with blond hair and dressed in light-brown woolen jacket and dark trousers, stood near the entrance. Dr. Hohberger, our attending physician, resembled more of a businessman than a doctor, but he was a kind and considerate gentleman. He aimed to avoid hospitalization to keep costs down.

He began with a swift but thorough checkup of both Mamatha's and my eyes, before turning his attention to Yogita, who was on Mamatha's lap. "This has a sedative. Please make sure she drinks this. It will make her sleepy and less cranky," he said, handing us a small plastic cup with about 5 ml of syrup resembling strawberry sauce. Yogita took it without hesitation.

A half an hour later, with Yogita mostly asleep, Dr. Hohberger administered two different eye drops and, using his ophthalmoscope, examined the interior of Yogita's eyes. After a few minutes of careful observation, he rose and invited us to follow him to his private office in a gentle yet firm tone.

"Conducting a comprehensive examination requires administering a brief anesthesia," he explained calmly.

Instantly, a surge of fear and panic rippled through me, manifesting as a flutter in the pit of my stomach. Glancing at Mamatha for her reaction, I asked in our native Kannada, "Enu maada du?" (What should we do?)

"Let them proceed, Mohan," Mamatha replied in English, her resolve firm despite the concern that flickered in her eyes.

I turned back to the doctor and gave my agreement.

His words carried seriousness as he continued. "This examination will necessitate hospitalization, and regrettably, I can only arrange the procedure for tomorrow morning."

He promptly instructed the nurse to conduct a comprehensive blood analysis for Yogita and to make the necessary arrangements for the procedure at the hospital. A mix of apprehension and hope filled the room as the details got sorted.

The following morning, we arrived at the hospital conveniently located across from the clinic. After giving Yogita the same strawberry-flavored sleeping medication, Dr. Hohberger's nurse took Yogita inside the operating room on a stretcher while we settled into the waiting area.

After what felt like an eternity, Dr. Hohberger emerged, pulled a chair from across the room, and sat down in front of us. The nurse followed, bringing our groggy daughter back to us. Yogita was twisting and turning, crying softly on the stretcher.

"She will be cranky for a while, but she'll fall asleep again soon," Dr. Hohberger reassured us.

A few minutes later, after hearing her parents' voices, Yogita did doze off again.

Mamatha and I sat before Dr. Hohberger, our anxiety palpable.

"What did the doctors in India tell you?" he asked.

"They prescribed glasses and told us to focus on bright, colorful objects, hoping it would stimulate her vision," I explained, my voice thick with frustration. "We've held toys with the brightest reds, blues, and yellows in front of her, but nothing seems to catch her attention. And every time we put the glasses on her, she pulls them off as if they're some kind of torture device. Honestly, we've given up on the glasses."

My words hung in the air, and a heavy silence followed.

Dr. Hohberger's brow furrowed as he sat back in his chair, his eyes fixed on the medical chart before him. A chill settled in the sterile room, the hum of the fluorescent lights above suddenly louder and oppressive.

I found myself gripping the armrests of the chair.

Dr. Hohberger glanced at Mamatha, then back at me, his eyes filled with profound sadness as though he wished he could soften the blow he was about to deliver. He drew a long breath before speaking, his voice softer now, more deliberate. "Yogita has retinal agenesis," he declared, his words cutting through the stillness like a blade.

CHAPTER 9

Shattered Hopes from Unseen Truths

(June 1990)

For a moment, I couldn't process what the doctor had said. I stared at him, confused.

Dr. Hohberger continued. "Yogita has never had optic nerves in her eyes. The optic nerve, which is an extension of the central nervous system, including the brain and spine, is missing. This condition was present at birth."

I had come to accept Yogita's blindness, but the revelation of a missing vital nerve connection to the brain was a terrifying shock.

How could the doctors in India have missed this, or did they withhold the information? The realization hit me, leaving me paralyzed by a storm of emotions—shock, terror, and uncontrollable sorrow. Inside, my mind screamed with two anguished questions: *How could the doctors overlook such a crucial detail? What unseen horrors are ahead for my precious daughter?*

Holding our daughter snugly in her arms, Mamatha turned to Dr. Hohberger and asked, "Can we fix that, Doctor? Perhaps with specialized glasses or through surgery?"

Her desperate and hopeful question only deepened my anguish.

Dr. Hohberger's response was gentle but final. "Glasses are mere adornments, futile in granting vision, Mrs. Rao. Yogita has been without optic nerves, the essential connection between the brain and the eyes, since birth. I'm afraid there's nothing we can do to restore her sight."

A painful lump lodged in my throat, rendering me speechless. I stood frozen, watching Mamatha's dreams shatter, her sorrow over Yogita's unending darkness reflected in every tear now streaming down her cheeks.

Dr. Hohberger bowed his head in compassionate understanding.

"Oh," I managed to utter hoarsely. It was the first time someone had directly confronted us with this devastating truth. A storm of rage, frustration, and helplessness surged through me. The doctors in India had deceived Mamatha and me. We had strapped glasses onto Yogita's head for months, clinging to false hopes and assurances that now made me feel like the biggest fool on the planet.

I closed my eyes and took a deep breath, trying to calm the turmoil inside. A thought suddenly flashed in my mind: *Had the doctors in India deliberately misled us into believing Yogita had some vision? Did they already know we would be left with shattered hopes from unseen truths?*

"Do you think our doctors did what they did to protect Mamatha's fragile postnatal mental state? Were they worried about her slipping into postpartum depression?" I asked Dr. Hohberger.

He responded with a noncommittal "Maybe."

"What should we do now, Doctor?" I asked, looking him straight in the eye.

"We need to determine if the abnormality is due to a genetic defect or a random developmental error," Dr. Hohberger explained.

"Does that mean if we have more children, they might have the same problem?" I asked, anxiety gripping my voice.

"Both of you will undergo investigations so we can study your genealogy. We'll conduct a chromosome test to identify any significant gene-related issues. By the way," he continued with a hint of pride,

"Mayo Clinic is the only place in the world where this advanced chromosome testing is available."

"Oh. Is it expensive?" I asked.

"Yes," he acknowledged, "but given your situation, we may consider it for our research purposes and not charge you the full amount. Our genetic counseling division will handle these investigations. Then, I will provide you with a detailed assessment of the likelihood of subsequent children having the same issue." Following a pause, Dr. Hohberger said, "I will take you to the genetic counselor now."

Feeling fear and discomfort, I looked at Mamatha for reassurance. She had managed to compose herself and showed no hesitation in pursuing a genetic prognosis. On many such occasions, Mamatha's boldness and courage had been the only driving force behind my strength.

The genetic counselor was a frail middle-aged man with sharp eyes, a long nose, and thinning white hair. He asked us to chart a detailed family tree to explore potential genealogical connections between Mamatha and me. After careful examination, he ultimately ruled out a direct familial connection.

A nurse arrived and took blood samples from Yogita, Mamatha, and me for chromosome testing. After she finished and told us the results would be available in a few days, we eagerly returned to our hotel.

The following days, Mamatha and I were restless, consumed by dread and anxiety. We wondered what we would do if the results revealed a problem with our chromosomes or if one of us carried a recessive gene. The uncertainty was overwhelming, and the pressure of the situation pressed heavily upon us.

When the results of the chromosome tests arrived, the office secretary called and asked us to return and discuss them with Dr. Hohberger.

We were tremendously relieved to learn they were normal.

The issue is not hereditary! I had many questions to ask for clarification. "So, what does this mean for us having more children?"

"I don't think you need to worry at all. I don't believe it will repeat in subsequent children," he answered reassuringly.

Mamatha glanced at me with a look that seemed to say, *I told you so.*

"We did not find anything abnormal in the chromosome tests, which means that Yogita's condition is not due to any major chromosomal changes. However, this test result does not completely rule out a specific recessive gene. Still, her problem is most unlikely to be genetic in origin. We cannot determine the exact cause of her condition either, though," he added.

At this point, I realized the forceps delivery could not be the cause of Yogita's blindness, which gave me some relief from my guilt for approving it. Yet, *could it have been the medications Mamatha took early on in her pregnancy?* I wondered. I chose not to ask that question, though, as I did not want Mamatha to shoulder any grief about that decision. There was nothing we could do about that now. Instead, I circled back to the most pressing question for both of us. "So, can we have more children without worrying about a recurrence?"

"Well, if it were due to a genetic defect, there would be a 25 percent chance of similar problems in subsequent children. Since it appears to be due to a random event in the womb, the risk is zero," Dr. Hohberger said and paused before continuing. "However, you should consult with an oculoplastic surgeon. Yogita might be a candidate for prosthetic eyes, also known as glass eyes."

I looked toward Mamatha to gauge her reaction. She didn't seem to be following what he meant. I couldn't let her see that my reaction was of complete anxiety. Thankfully, Dr. Hohberger, being an especially kind and culturally sensitive individual, asked if Mamatha would like to take Yogita to the peaceful waiting lounge while we discussed the logistics of what was next.

Mamatha, accustomed to this, went without hesitation.

I braced myself in the chair and asked him, "Why would she need glass eyes?"

"The oculoplastic surgeon will be able to guide you more on this decision, but I need to tell you that it is rare for children with disabilities like Yogita to have just one handicap," he said, his tone unwavering.

"Does she have other problems?" I asked, struggling to swallow the lump forming in my throat.

He was looking at his notes again. "There is a small risk that Yogita may have a tumor in her left eye. To confirm this possibility, we would need to remove her eyeball for examination and replace it with a prosthetic. It would be wise to do this with both of her eyes. Without the prosthetics, enucleation alone would prevent her eye sockets from growing properly, leaving her with permanently closed, tiny eyes. The prosthetics will help to preserve aesthetic appearance and avoid disfigurement."

Dr. Hohberger's gaze stayed fixed to his notes as though he could not bear to meet mine.

The idea of Yogita losing her eyes in such a brutal way was a torment that clawed at my soul, an excruciating anguish I could hardly endure. "No," I choked out, my voice trembling with desperation and fear.

"But keeping her eyes could significantly aid our research," he said, maintaining a clinical detachment from the emotional turmoil engulfing me.

The word escaped me again in a broken hiccup. "No."

Silence fell between us, heavy with the impact of a decision I could not bear to make. After a long moment, he responded with gentle acknowledgment, "I understand."

Dr. Hohberger got up to shake my hand and kindly offered more of his time should we need to discuss things with him further.

Desperate to escape the suffocating situation, I sought refuge in hurried steps toward the lounge where Mamatha and Yogita waited. I masked my shattered emotions with a façade of urgency. I stifled my sobs, disguising them as coughs as I raced away from the horrifying meeting, hiding tears threatening to betray my broken heart.

"Mohan, what happened?" Mamatha's voice trembled with concern.

"He wanted to discuss artificial eyes that might help her see in the future," I lied, my heart heavy with the burden of deceit.

Her concern shifted, turning to hopeful yet naive optimism. "Yogita will find independence once she speaks," Mamatha tried to reassure herself, clinging to a fragile hope.

"Yes," I echoed, concealing the bitter truth and locking away my crushing despair. I lacked the strength and courage to discuss with Mamatha the prospect of donating Yogita's eyeballs or the potential for other forthcoming anomalies.

I went through the elaborate discharge formalities, which included counseling from an expert who emphasized the importance of early intervention and specialized services for Yogita.

Mamatha was quiet as we walked back to the motel. Once there, she asked for some time alone and went out for a walk. She returned after an hour, her face streaked with tears.

"What happened, Mamatha?" I asked, concerned.

"What will we do now that Yogita is definitely blind?" she asked. "I went to the church we saw the other day. There was a mass going on. Afterward, I approached the pastor and asked him whose fault it was that my daughter was born blind. He asked me what I meant by *whose fault it was*, then said that the question implies someone did it on purpose—which, of course, is ridiculous. He said, 'If you must place fault, place it on the society that refuses to see your child as a child, but as a problem and a burden.'"

Though spoken through tears, her words carried a bitter truth that stung deeply. The pastor's insight was a harsh reminder of the societal challenges we would face, but it was also a call to shift our focus from seeking blame or cures to advocating for our child's acceptance and support.

Mamatha continued. "I then asked him what the Bible had to say about my child. He quoted some verse, saying, 'it was so all His works might be displayed.'"

"What does that even mean?" I asked, bewildered.

She shrugged, tears rolling down her cheeks, unable to offer any clarity.

That evening, Dr. Murali, Vasu's class friend who had helped me make the appointments and remained in touch throughout our stay in Rochester, called to check on Yogita's prognosis.

"Murali, they say Yogita was born without optic nerves in both eyes," I blurted out, overcome with emotion.

There was a brief pause. Then he gently suggested, "Mohan, why don't you get a second opinion?"

"But isn't Mayo the best in the world?" I asked, still grappling with the news.

"It is, but considering the distance you've traveled, it's worth consulting Pittsburgh Children's Hospital, one of the top pediatric facilities here."

Mamatha interrupted. "I don't want Yogita to endure another eye exam!"

In the same frame of mind, I agreed with Mamatha. Nevertheless, the following day, I requested Mayo to forward the reports to Murali so he could review things while we made arrangements to visit him in Pittsburgh.

Our experience at Mayo left us disheartened, yet we found solace in the small comforts—a talking alarm clock, for example, that a nurse suggested to help Mamatha with Yogita's schedule.

Within a day, we flew to Pittsburgh, where Murali greeted us warmly, dressed sharply in a suit, a far cry from the casual figure I knew back home. His house, nestled in a quiet suburban neighborhood, felt like a sanctuary after the emotional turmoil of Rochester.

Murali's wife, Mani, welcomed us with a big smile, wide open arms, and the comforting aroma of South Indian dishes, offering us a respite from the relentless tension. Their lively and affectionate daughter, Antha, quickly accepted Yogita, who was curious and intrigued by their interactions. For the first time in weeks, we felt at ease.

Later, Murali reiterated the importance of a second opinion, and after some thought, Mamatha and I agreed.

At the Pittsburgh Children's Hospital, a team of specialists confirmed what we already knew: Yogita's condition was a rare, random developmental error. Still, hearing the words again, especially from such renowned experts, gave us a sense of closure.

On Yogita's first birthday, the 18th of June, Murali and Mani took us to a hibachi restaurant, where we shared a bittersweet meal, knowing our return to India was approaching. Murali, learning Yogita loved the water, suggested she buy Yogita a small inflatable pool to bring home with us—a heartwarming gift.

As our British Airways flight took off toward London, I looked out the little window at the clouds that appeared like white cotton candy. Overall, the kindness and acceptance we experienced in the U.S. brought a measure of peace to Mamatha and me. We especially found comfort in how people treated Yogita with normalcy, without pity or judgment. Likewise, the flight crew was kind and accommodating, providing a bassinet where Yogita slept peacefully. I soon followed suit and drifted off.

I woke up from a jolt of turbulence. Yogita barely stirred, and Mamatha remained asleep, a blanket pulled over her face. The steady hum of the plane's engines filled the background. Quietly, I made my way to the flight crew for a snack. As I munched on a cookie that reminded me of my mother's homemade ones, though not quite as good, my thoughts wandered to my past, Yogita's future, and our journey together.

I thought of the giant brown hardbound ledger my father used as a calendar for family events, which chronicled my arrival into this world: "Saturday, January 18, 1958, a male child born at 10:30 p.m., weighing 6.6 pounds." Yet, in a peculiar twist, my official secondary school leaving certificate (SSLC) listed my birth date as May 18, 1957. My father had enrolled me in primary school, a year older on paper than I truly was, so that I could qualify for a crucial district exam. It was a clever move, though it created an ongoing contradiction in my life that I now understood on a deeper level. This discrepancy had always intrigued me and felt like a symbolic reminder of the many unpredictable turns life could take. *How will Yogita's educational path be different from mine? Will she even be able to go to school?*

As a newborn, I had been frail and often sickly. My mother used to tell me how she feared I might not survive my first few years. At just one year old, I had battled diphtheria and typhoid, leading to a month-long hospital stay after a relapse. Only with the help of newly-introduced baby food from Glaxo did I begin to thrive, earning the nickname "Bun" from the hospital staff.

Looking at Yogita, the same age I was when I was sickly, I could better understand the concerns my mother must have faced back then. However, I didn't have memories of living with my parents for most of my childhood. After staying with them at their factory until I was two, they took me to live with my six brothers, my sister Vanaja, and my grandmother. Only after my father retired and we moved to Sita Vilas did I spend significant time with my parents again. Despite the unconventional arrangement, I never felt unloved. My family's presence was constant, and I always felt surrounded by care.

My mother, especially, had been kind to me, as I was her youngest child and bore a strong resemblance to her. Yet, regrettably, as a teenager, I didn't fully reciprocate her affection, which has been one of my enduring regrets. In her last days, as she battled dementia, I did little to support her. Looking back, I wish I had spent more time truly understanding my mother and bonding with her while I had the chance.

I checked on Yogita, who was still sleeping soundly as the rhythm of the plane's engine hummed away, and thought about my mother's many sacrifices. She had been a remarkable woman in many ways. Her Sunday ghee preparations, Sindhi phulkas with potato bhaji, and delicious shortbread cookies, were unmatched. She learned baking in Aruvankadu near Ooty. She would often survey sand dunes to get the finest sand for baking the butter cookies. She needed the fine sand to ensure uniform baking. We did not have ovens, and only very fine sand could be heated up to 180 degrees centigrade to bake cookies at home. These small acts of love were her way of nurturing us.

I looked over at Mamatha, whose love was undoubtedly the guiding light for Yogita and me, no matter the challenges ahead. As the plane descended into Heathrow, I couldn't help but think about how our journey was far from over. While Yogita's future was uncertain, so, too, was my ability to navigate it.

CHAPTER 10

My Darkest Moment

(Yogita: Age 1 - 2)

After a brief layover at Heathrow, we boarded our flight back to Bangalore, with a quick stop in Mumbai. The moment we stepped out of the airport and onto the bustling streets of India, it was undeniable that we had plunged back into the heart of our vibrant world. The air was thick with the familiar scents of spices and street food, and the atmosphere hummed with life. India's kaleidoscope of colors greeted us at every turn—trucks painted in bold electric blues and fiery reds rumbled down the roads, their intricate designs storytelling in themselves. Fruit and flower carts brimmed with vivid hues, while women in radiant sarees moved gracefully through the crowd, their bangles glittering like sunlight on water. It was a feast for the senses, a living tapestry of culture and chaos, that welcomed us home.

We spent the night in Bangalore with Mamatha's parents before returning to Mysore the next evening. The weight of Yogita's diagnosis hung heavily, bound to our exhausting journey across the U.S. through hospitals and relentless financial strain. Medical expenses had surged to a staggering $50,000, and for the first time, I faced personal financial hardship. Born with a silver spoon, I had never truly felt the burden of scarcity—but even privilege could not shield me from life's harshest blows. Very little was left from my partition settlement as I had invested most of it into my pharmaceutical and food ventures, which, while they still held promise, had yet to yield any profit.

My brothers, once my confidants and comrades, offered no reprieve from my financial misery. The stark realization of the finite nature of both familial and financial ties was a bitter pill to swallow. For the first time in my journey as an adult and businessman, I was at the mercy of a private financier.

Navigating these financial uncertainties felt like learning to stand again, unsure and unsteady. I chose not to discuss it with Mamatha, aware of the stark contrast between our financial worlds. Her father, a deputy manager at a large defense factory, lived modestly, and I didn't want to weigh her down with our financial burdens.

Meanwhile, back in our cozy home in Gokulam, Yogita was also finding her balance. Within four months of our return, she began standing on her own, her wobbly steps mirroring the uncertainty I felt in my struggles. Each time she tried, she'd get confused just how it was supposed to work, yet she remained undeterred. Adding to the challenges of caring for her, despite our best efforts to keep her active during the day, her long naps persisted, leaving her wide awake at night—a rhythm disrupting our lives.

Our fancy talking alarm clock was not solving that problem. After reading the materials from the Mayo Clinic, I learned that Yogita's circadian rhythm and sleep cycle were disrupted due to her inability to experience light. So we would stay awake in shifts, always alert, fearing she might harm herself as she tried to move about, lost in her world. Sleep deprivation began to sap my alertness, making me irritable at the office.

While Mamatha had very few relatives, I had an extended family of nearly thirty members. I decided to bring Yogita into the fold, hoping her slightly older cousins would visit and spend time with her, helping to keep her awake during the day.

I wrote a note to all the family members that went like this:

"Hi, I am Yogita, your cousin. You all see through your eyes, but I see through my fingers and feel through my tongue. I know I may seem strange to you, but please talk to me. Please hand me different textures and items so I can feel and understand them. Please don't ignore me."

Since the internet did not yet exist, I had to make typed copies and distribute them to all my nieces and nephews. The younger ones began interacting with Yogita, sitting with her and trying to play with toys. But it was difficult for them, as she never responded or reacted to their affectionate gestures. She did, however, love the inflatable mini swimming pool that Murali and his wife gifted us. She spent many evenings happily playing in the water.

When Yogita was about fifteen months old, I received a call from Mamatha late one afternoon while I was at the office. "Mohan, Turry just took her first solid step! I think she's figured it out!" Mamatha's voice was bubbling with excitement.

A surge of joy rushed through me. "I can't wait to see her walk," I replied, immediately pushing my chair back, my mind already focused on home.

As soon as I entered the house, I saw Mamatha squatting on the floor, her arms outstretched around Yogita as she took her first independent steps. She balanced precariously with her hands in the air. I sat a few feet away, watching in awe as she toddled cautiously from Mamatha's steady hands to mine, each step deliberate and filled with the wonder of discovery. That moment filled me with indescribable pride.

Soon after, Yogita found her own method of navigating the world. She began holding onto the walls, inching along them as she walked the perimeter of the rooms. Curious, Yogita cautiously explored the house like a new adventurer, never letting go of her makeshift guide. For weeks, she clung to the walls, uncertain yet determined. One day, her curiosity led her to a discovery—by holding onto the drapes, she could make it from the veranda to the front door. Unfortunately, this also meant pulling the curtains down along the way.

To help her gain confidence, I often carried her on my back, guiding her tiny hand to trace the walls with her right hand while her left hand wandered, feeling the textures of objects nearby. It was our way of exploring together, and I cherished those moments.

Once she gained confidence, there was no stopping her. Yogita became a whirlwind of exploration, especially in the kitchen. She delighted in knocking utensils off the counter, turning on switches just to hear the clicks and hums, and even inserting her fingers into electrical outlets, forcing me to cover them up. Outside, she would eagerly feel the tires of the car and—much to our horror—lick them, only to grimace at the taste.

She turned bathroom taps on with glee and wandered through the house endlessly, her arms outstretched like the white canes used by blind adults. Feeding her became an adventure in itself; we had to follow her from room to room, trying to coax her to eat while she explored her surroundings.

We continued to try to socialize Yogita as it was a top priority for her development. At family gatherings, Yogita would find the nearest wall and press her palms against it, tracing the edges of the room. Her tiny fingers glided over every surface as she mapped out her environment. Occasionally, she would stumble over a table or sofa, her unsteady legs betraying her curiosity. Mamatha and I would trail behind her, always watching, always on guard. We silently hoped someone might offer to take over briefly to give us a moment to rest. But no one did.

For those around us, Yogita was unlike any other child, and this difference made most people uneasy. A few brave souls attempted to interact with her, but when she didn't respond as expected, they quickly withdrew, unsure of how to continue. Her developmental delays made communication challenging—she never spoke the typical first words like "Mom" or "Dad." Occasionally, she would murmur "Mum-Mum" when hungry or call me "Didil-Didil," but these words were rare and inconsistent.

Though I had come to terms with the reality that Yogita would never see and would lag behind other children, a small part of me clung to a faint, persistent hope not based on solid expectations. I held an unspoken dream that one day, science would provide a solution—a breakthrough that could give her sight through electronic or artificial means. I carried this dream as a way to maintain the positivity I was learning to cultivate, though the task of integrating Yogita into the world remained uniquely challenging. Her comfort was deeply tied to Mamatha and me, making her world feel safe.

Whenever I was home, she could instantly recognize me by the sound of my footsteps or the smell of my cologne. She would latch onto me, craving my attention. Unlike Mamatha, I was more lenient, indulging her every whim, which only deepened her attachment to me. She also found joy in unusual things—like empty cassette covers. She'd open and close them for hours, utterly absorbed in the simple action. She would even continue late into the night, lost in her repetitive motion. Doctors suggested she might be mildly autistic, given her preference for sensory play and the fact that she never crawled like other babies.

One morning, I observed Mamatha who was ever so diligent in taking special care of Yogita's hair. She had carefully laid out her comb and brush on the small wooden table beside our bed. Yogita, now sitting on the bed, was already in her usual spot, her small fingers touching the familiar texture of the blanket.

"Time for Turry's ponytails," Mamatha said softly, her tone full of warmth. She gently approached Yogita with the brush, her hands steady but filled with anticipation.

Yogita, sensing the familiar routine, tensed up. As soon as Mamatha's fingers brushed against her hair, Yogita's body went rigid. Her tiny hands shot out to grab the brush, pulling it away from Mamatha's grasp. She brought it to her mouth, exploring the bristles with her tongue. A muffled, frustrated noise escaped her lips.

Observing from the doorway, I said, "Mamatha, she really doesn't like it when you brush her hair," my heart aching at the sight. "Do you think it's more than just dislike? Maybe it's something we should talk to her doctors about."

Mamatha glanced at me with a mix of concern and resolve. "I know, but it's part of her routine. I have to keep the knots out of her hair."

With a sigh, Mamatha tried again, but Yogita was even more determined this time. She yanked off the hairbands with a swift, practiced motion and shook her head vigorously. Her hair, now a wild cascade, covered her face.

"Maybe this is her way of controlling her environment," I suggested, stepping closer to offer my support.

Mamatha nodded, her eyes filled with a blend of frustration and understanding. "It's possible. She has her ways of showing what she needs or doesn't need." Despite the struggle, Mamatha took a deep breath and gently pulled Yogita into a hug. "All right, sweet Turry, let's leave the hair for today. How about we play with your favorite cassette covers instead?"

Yogita's tense posture relaxed into Mamatha's embrace when she heard the mention of her beloved toy. She reached out, eager to explore the familiar texture of the cassette cover, her focus shifting away from the hairbrush.

Watching Yogita engrossed in her new activity reminded us of the many layers of her world. We knew that understanding her needs and preferences, even in these small moments, was crucial to helping her navigate her life with as much comfort and joy as possible.

There were so many moments we needed to pivot what we did in real time to be more understanding of where Yogita was coming from. One morning, when Mamatha and I were still in bed, Yogita approached us with toothpaste smeared all over her mouth, having squeezed an entire tube and painted her face white. Other times, we encouraged Yogita to feed herself things like rice pudding. Despite our efforts, she often preferred staying hungry to eating independently.

Toilet training was yet another challenge, though Yogita eventually did learn to signal her needs with the word "ussa." Public outings were generally manageable, but once, at a dinner party, Yogita relieved herself in her pants as a form of protest, sensing our brief distraction. This incident highlighted the ongoing struggle to balance her needs with public situations.

By two years old, Yogita showed minimal improvement in self-help skills and expression. Our dilemma often centered on whether to push her harder or prioritize her comfort. After much consideration, we chose to prioritize her peace of mind, working closely with the Blind Association of India to enhance her self-help skills without adding undue stress.

As our home life demands persisted, so did the sleepless nights, making me perpetually drowsy and affecting my ability to work.

On a Monday, Venkatesh startled me as I dozed off in my swivel chair, feet propped up on the table. "Sorry, Sir. Were you sleeping?" asked my tall, dark, ever-smiling C.O.O. as I groggily straightened up.

"That's okay. What is it?"

"The executive engineer from the Electricity Board is here. You asked me to inform you when he arrived for the investigation."

I grimaced and wiped my face with a handkerchief. "Send him in," I instructed, "and please ask Vatsala to prepare a strong coffee for me and a regular one for him."

Moments later, the executive engineer entered my office.

"Good morning," I greeted him.

He didn't bother to reciprocate. His face was full of self-importance, radiating the power and position he enjoyed.

I felt an immediate surge of repulsion and launched into my explanation, telling him how my electrician was unaware the energy meter wiring had come loose due to faulty installation by the department.

"You should have informed the department at once," he said.

"We wrote to the department a month ago."

"You can't just write a letter and go silent. Do you know not getting your meter fixed is a punishable offense under the law?"

I lost my cool. "We have not tampered with the meter or the panel board. What do you expect from us? Did you think I should come to your office, hold your hand, and drag you here?"

The engineer was visibly shocked. He glared at me, got up, and left.

Thanks to my outburst, we had to run our factory using our captive power plant—a generator—for a good fifteen days. It took over two weeks, a favorable word from the retired chairman of K.E.B., and a basket full of fruits to sort out the issue.

Almost constantly, my eyes felt heavy. Frequent headaches numbed my brain, and I regularly fell asleep at my desk.

Yogita's blindness and her slow cognitive development were severely testing our mental and physical endurance, all while my business career was at its nadir.

Desperately wanting to share my struggles, I blurted out my sorrows to my brother Venkatesh one afternoon.

"My God, Mohan. If I were you, I would have committed suicide by now!" he exclaimed.

I didn't know what to think about that, let alone what to say.

On one particular Sunday, I took Yogita to my brother's house to give Mamatha some alone time. Everyone was busy in the kitchen while I followed Yogita around in her new environment.

As Yogita wandered through the house, I trailed behind, watching her trace the unfamiliar walls, cautiously step up the staircase, and finally explore the upstairs bedroom. I stayed close, carefully guiding her, protecting her from any danger that might cause her to stumble. In the bedroom, she found a hairbrush on my nephew's bed and clutched it tightly, a small treasure in her little hands.

As we made our way downstairs, her curiosity shifted to the wooden banister, which she began to lick, refusing to budge. My concern for her safety grew—germs, infections, the unknown risks. Without thinking, frustration surged, and before I even registered what I was doing, I struck her on the head to get her to stop licking the banister.

The moment my hand landed, everything changed. Yogita stumbled and fell, and I was left staring at the aftermath of my loss of control. I immediately scooped up her tiny, trembling body. I sensed her fear, knowing I had shaken her trust in me. She clung to me, whimpering, unsure of what had just happened.

Without returning to the kitchen, I quickly left the house, carrying Yogita to the car with the impact of what I had done crashing over me. My guilt was immediate and immense like a tidal wave pulling me under. How could I, her father, the one meant to protect her, be the cause of her pain? I held her close, my heart breaking as she continued trembling in my arms, starkly reminding me of her innocence. I had failed her.

The drive home was agonizing. I was aware of Yogita sitting in the back in her little car seat as tears blurred my vision, running freely down my cheeks. I struggled to face the reality of my actions. I was consumed by remorse so deep that words could never express my pain and self-loathing. I repeatedly struck my face as if I could somehow punish myself enough to erase the harm I had caused, even while knowing that I could not undo what I had done. It was the only time I was grateful she could not see me—in my misery.

What good was all that reading and work on self-development in my darkest moment of exhaustion? To this day, the memory of that event remains vivid, etched into my mind like a wound that refuses to heal. While time has passed, the ache has never dulled. It serves as a constant reminder of my human flaws.

In the wake of that painful day, I made a vow, a sacred promise to myself and Yogita. I swore I would never allow fatigue or stress to dictate my actions again, no matter what tests arose or how difficult the circumstances became. I promised to shield her from my darkness, to be the steady comfort in her life, a pillar of patience and compassion. Every moment she wandered in her world, I would be there, guiding her. Never again would my frustration lead to her suffering.

CHAPTER 11

Focus Shift

(Yogita: Age 2)

I learned of Helen Keller's book, *The Story of My Life*,[c] and O'Sullivan's method of teaching Helen Keller to speak by having her touch her face, feel the vibrations from her nose, lips, and larynx, and then talk. It inspired me to try a similar approach with Yogita. I thought Yogita might be unable to produce words involving her lips because she couldn't see others doing it and thus missed out on uttering words like "Baa," "Maa," or "Pa."

Mamatha and I discussed this approach at length. She first tried placing Yogita's fingers gently on her lips while saying "Appa" loudly and slowly, with exaggerated movements. But Yogita did not respond.

When I said "Amma" several times, exaggerating the lip movements with one of Yogita's hands on my throat and two fingers on my lips, that also did not work.

Taking a leaf from O'Sullivan's methods, I carried Yogita to a tap. Just like O'Sullivan, I placed her left hand under the running water and put the fingers of her right hand on my lips, loudly uttering "water." She did not understand. I tried this several times, and eventually, she pulled away her fingers and, making a hissing noise, went off to walk along the nearest wall.

Mamatha and I were keen on introducing Yogita to as many different environments, smells, textures, and people as we could. She loved smooth finishes, disliked rough or hard surfaces, and preferred toys that made melodious sounds, vibrated, or emitted pleasant smells. We informed people she was about to meet that she could not make eye contact, so "please touch her gently and speak to her by name."

One weekend, we took Yogita to my eldest brother Guru's house.

"How are you, Mona? Have you come for financial help?" he asked, to my shock and sadness.

"No, Guru. I'm bringing Yogita to all my brothers' houses to introduce her to new surroundings and people."

Seeing the effort I was putting in, Guru suggested, "Mona, I believe there is an excellent residential school for blind girls in Poona. Why don't you consider sending Yogita there?"

The thought of being away from Yogita profoundly saddened me. My heart ached at the mere idea. I gathered myself and replied, "I will discuss it with Mamatha, Guru." I glanced at Mamatha and immediately recognized her discomfort.

As soon as we returned home, Mamatha blurted out, "We are not putting her in a blind school, Mohan." Her tone was firm and adamant.

Around that time, my eldest sister, Padma, who was twenty-one years older than me, came to visit. I was born the same year as her first son, my nephew Konde. As a mother of four adults, Padma tried hard to help Yogita feel comfortable. Eventually, Yogita sat on her lap.

After failing to elicit any meaningful response from Yogita, my sister turned to me and said, "Mohan, for a child of her age, her inability to express herself is very troubling. Why don't you take her to a speech and hearing center and get her assessed?"

"Her hearing is excellent, Padma. Some children take a little longer."

"Still, take her to one," Padma insisted. "She's not even blabbering."

The following week, we took Yogita to the All-India Institute of Speech and Hearing (AIISH). Recognized as one of the best institutions in the country for children with speech and hearing impairments,

AIISH was just three kilometers from our home. Set on a lush, thirty-two-acre campus, the institute was renowned for its eleven departments equipped with state-of-the-art facilities. They offered clinical services for a wide range of communication disorders, including speech, language, hearing, and swallowing.

Dr. Prathibha Karanth, an expert in speech disorders, greeted us. She took Yogita in her arms and whispered in her ears, but Yogita did not respond.

"Does she have any hearing problems?" Dr. Karanth inquired.

Both Mamatha and I shook our heads. "She is very fond of music and can hear very well," Mamatha replied.

"We will conduct a hearing test, followed by a speech assessment." Dr. Karanth said. "Does she engage in any repetitive activities?"

Mamatha and I thought for a moment.

"She keeps playing with cassette cases and sometimes sways back and forth by herself," Mamatha confirmed.

"We will need to rule out autism," Dr. Karanth said. "We'll assess her further."

Two young women in white coats, who appeared to be Dr. Karanth's students, took Yogita into a room. Yogita started wailing, so Mamatha and I rushed in to console her, giving her an empty cassette tape cover to play with. Once she quieted down, they asked us to leave and closed the door, observing her through a glass pane on the other side of the room. A man seated at a large console put on his headphones and began playing various sounds through the speakers from different directions, noting Yogita's head movements.

"Her hearing is excellent," Dr. Karanth announced. "We should start her on speech therapy right away." They did a further evaluation to identify if she was autistic, but as she didn't fall under the normal parameters of testing, they could only say it was inconclusive.

We began taking Yogita for daily speech therapy sessions, hoping the increased frequency would help her progress. The patient, dedicated therapist spent countless hours with her, trying every method she could. One day, she placed a tennis ball in front of Yogita, holding her finger gently to her lips, and said, "Baaallll." Instead of mimicking the word, Yogita began to feel and taste the ball, her fascination for textures overriding any interest in speech. After three months and several therapists, each bringing their unique approach but barely getting her to sit still for even a minute, there was no change—not even a single word.

Yogita remained silent, lost in her sensory explorations. Frustrated and anxious, I decided to act. I called Dr. Karanth, the director of the All-India Institute of Speech and Hearing. "I'm really worried about Yogita's progress," I told her, my voice strained.

"I understand," Dr. Karanth replied gently. "I, too, am not satisfied with the results. After three months of intensive therapy, we should have seen at least some progress by now. It's time we assess her cognitive development."

The next three days were filled with tests. Yogita was observed, measured, and evaluated in every way possible. Finally, Mamatha and I sat down with Dr. Karanth to hear the results.

Dr. Karanth began, her voice carefully measured. "I'm afraid Yogita is mildly retarded." (This term would never be used today, but that is how it was presented to us.) "Though she's two, her cognitive development is that of a three-month-old, and her comprehension aligns with a six-month-old child."

Mamatha broke down immediately, her quiet sobs filling the room.

I squeezed Mamatha's arm to comfort her while suppressing the ache building inside me. "So, what now, Dr. Karanth?" I asked, trying to keep my voice steady.

"I suggest appointing a highly qualified speech therapist for Yogita—someone experienced enough to tailor the therapy to her needs. It may cost more, but she deserves the best."

I glanced at Mamatha, who wiped her tears and gave a hopeful nod. "That would be wonderful," I said.

"I have someone in mind," Dr. Karanth continued. "Dr. Usha is working on her Ph.D. in speech therapy and has over five years of experience. She's one of the best. I'll call her right away."

Eager to begin this new phase of therapy, we went to Usha's house the next morning, just a short walk from the institute. Usha, a bespectacled woman with an air of professionalism, lived with her husband (an architect) and their four-year-old son.

"Oh, come on in. You must be Mamatha, and this must be Yogita," Usha greeted us warmly, reaching out to pinch Yogita's cheek.

Yogita, however, did not respond, as usual. Her indifference to new people was no longer surprising to us.

After a few weeks of intense speech therapy, Usha's enthusiasm waned. The hours spent trying to coax even a single word from Yogita took their toll. She would patiently place Yogita's small fingers on her lips and slowly pronounce words like "ball," but Yogita's only response was to explore the sensation of the sounds rather than repeat them. Usha's patience, although vast, was showing cracks, and Yogita's frustration became more apparent.

Sensing the need for a break, I decided it was time for us to take a vacation. I booked a five-night stay at The Leela Resorts in Goa for the three of us. It had been nearly two years since Mamatha and I had taken a holiday. Although finances were tight, I borrowed money for this indulgence, hoping a change in environment might help us all recharge.

Leela Resorts was a beautiful escape, with a private beach along the Arabian Sea and serene waterways crisscrossing the grounds. I had hoped the long day of travel would tire Yogita out, and she might finally sleep through the night in this new, peaceful setting. But Yogita remained unshaken in her routine. On the first night, well before midnight, she was wide awake, her little hands exploring every corner of the unfamiliar room, her face lighting up with her usual sounds of curiosity—hissing and cooing whenever she encountered something new.

As the clock struck midnight, Yogita's playful squeals reached a crescendo, and suddenly, a loud scream echoed from the room next to ours. The French couple staying there was clearly not amused by our nocturnal child. We could hear the husband's voice attempting to console his distressed wife, and amidst the angry French outbursts, I distinctly heard "merde" several times.

Their frustration boiled over into more swearing, and with only a thin wall separating us, we had no choice but to endure their complaints. *If only they knew Yogita's challenges. Perhaps they wouldn't be so loud or unkind.*

The change of scenery did us some good, and we returned to Mysore a few days later, as rested as we could be.

For the following two months, Usha tried her best to make Yogita imitate her words. She spent countless hours working with our daughter, guiding Yogita's fingers to her lips and repeating simple sounds. Still, no words came.

One evening, as we sat together, Mamatha voiced her concerns. "Mohan, we have to start teaching Yogita to do things on her own. We can't keep making life easier for her. If she doesn't learn now, how will she manage later? She must learn to eat, drink, and even go to the toilet by herself."

"I agree," I said, nodding. "We have to make her self-reliant and more responsive to the world around her. It's not enough to just get by."

Mamatha sighed, her love for Yogita evident in her reluctance. "But she doesn't even eat on her own, Mohan. How can we make her do it?"

"We need to be firm," I replied. "Let's start small. We won't feed her for a few hours and see if hunger pushes her to try. We'll put a bowl of her favorite pudding in front of her and guide her hand with the spoon. She'll learn if we keep at it."

Mamatha hesitated but eventually agreed. And so, we began. For weeks, we pushed Yogita gently but firmly, guiding her hands and trying to make her feed herself. The process was slow, but Mamatha's persistence paid off over time. Little by little, Yogita learned to drink by herself, which was a small victory in our long journey of teaching her independence.

Mamatha and I grew increasingly uncomfortable with how society judged Yogita. At a newly opened Krishna temple down the street, an older lady asked Mamatha, "Has she been like this since birth?" Mamatha, trying to shield herself from the scrutiny, pretended not to hear.

Despite the sympathy and compliments on Yogita's beauty, it often felt as though people saw her attractiveness as a tragic contrast to her blindness rather than a simple, genuine compliment. The world seemed to overlook that Yogita had no visual benchmarks; she had never seen a flower or a landscape. Yet, she found profound joy in the sounds of nature, music, and melody, finding beauty in ways that many others might not.

One of the most significant lessons I was learning from Yogita was how my previous notions about people with disabilities were rooted in fear, ignorance, and prejudice rather than reality. I had pitied them for what they lacked without recognizing their capacity for joy. Mamatha and I were committed to ensuring Yogita's participation in mainstream society despite the significant barriers posed by societal attitudes and the stigma surrounding disabilities.

To help Mamatha and me understand the challenges faced by parents of blind and intellectually challenged children, Atma Ram Rao connected us with Rajan, an IAS officer who had recently relocated to Mysore. Rajan, a man of intellect in his forties, and his elegant wife, Anasuya, welcomed us into their world.

As they introduced their sons, Ganesh (six) and Vikram (eight), both blind but appearing healthy in every other way, I concealed my shock and greeted them with a polite, "Hello, boys."

"Why don't you sing them a song?" Rajan asked his sons.

The boys sang a Malayalam song in perfect harmony. Their performance was exceptional, but what struck me most was the complete absence of sorrow or remorse in the couple's eyes. The depth of strength I found in their serene demeanor made me feel ashamed and embarrassed about the despair that Mamatha and I initially felt, in stark contrast to their home, which radiated fulfillment and joy. Their example jolted us into a profound realization: our perspective on life's challenges needed a radical shift.

Our encounter with Rajan's family became a turning point. It lifted the heaviness from our hearts and broadened our view beyond our immediate struggles. We came to understand that our perception of Yogita's condition needed recalibration.

"Mohan, wasn't it Helen Keller who said, 'I cried because I had no shoes until I met a man who had no feet'?"[5] Mamatha asked.

"Hmmm," I responded, feeling the same way.

"We should stop treating Yogita's condition as a major tragedy."

I had complained about having a child who could not see until I met parents who had two blind children.

As the months passed, more transformations took hold within me. Joy, which I once feared, slowly became my companion. The sinister thought that happiness was merely a prelude to tragedy started to ease. Mamatha's unwavering positivity and Yogita's innocent happiness began to lift the mental fog clouding my mind. I realized that happiness was not a harbinger of tragedy but a gift—one to be cherished.

With that focus shift came a change in how I envisioned Yogita's future. Instead of focusing solely on her limitations, I began to see the possibilities ahead for her. I wanted to give her every advantage, to open up a world where she could thrive and not just adapt. As those thoughts formed, I considered something I hadn't before. *What if living in the U.S. could offer Yogita a better life?*

CHAPTER 12

Sights Set on America

(1991)

During one of Yogita's naps, Mamatha and I began discussing the possibility of moving to the United States. While India offered the comfort of cultural familiarity, extended family support, and more manageable financial demands, the challenges of raising a blind child there were overwhelming. Stigma, misconceptions, and a lack of accessible infrastructure severely hindered any path to independence for Yogita.

India lagged in inclusive education, specialized resources, and societal awareness. In contrast, the U.S. had an environment that fostered inclusion, encouraging blind children to participate in everyday activities, along with specialized schools and programs that nurtured a sense of belonging.

"Overall, I think the U.S. is the best place for Yogita. I've always dreamt of studying there, too. Do you remember my friend Azhar? He's doing his Ph.D. and teaching at Kennesaw State University. He keeps telling me that, for someone like me, the U.S. is perfect for advanced studies," I told Mamatha.

"You want to take up studies now, Mona?" Mamatha asked, surprised.

"I'm thirty-three, Mamatha. There's still time for me to take the GRE, or GMAT, and pursue postgraduate studies at a good university in the U.S."

"And what about your businesses here, Mohan? Are you really ready to give it all up and move?"

"Yes. I'll sell the property on Devaraj Urs Road to clear Arvee's loans. It's the only asset I have left after the family partition. We'll take whatever remains and start fresh."

Mamatha thought for a moment. "Yogita would definitely benefit from the special education and the more inclusive culture in the U.S."

"Exactly," I said, nodding. "We'll need about 5,000 USD a month for two years, plus my college fees. If I sell the property, we should have enough left after paying off the loan."

Mamatha was quiet, considering the numbers. "Mohan, we're fortunate to have our own businesses. That gives us the freedom to make these choices. But maybe you should take another trip to the U.S. first, and gather more information about schools and programs for blind children. I know they're much more integrated into society over there."

I consulted a lawyer who had practiced in the U.S. about the possibility of taking Mamatha and Yogita with me as a student. We explored several options, but all required close to half a million U.S. dollars. Raising that amount seemed daunting, but I began brainstorming ways to make it possible.

In the evenings, I spent several weeks preparing for the GMAT and TOEFL (Test of English as a Foreign Language), managing to score 560 and 600, respectively. Encouraged by my results, I started applying to advanced management programs at schools like Carnegie Mellon, Rutgers, and Buffalo. The process took time—each correspondence with the U.S. took about a month—and three months flew by as I submitted application forms and completed all the formalities.

One day, Mamatha, observing my dedication, asked, "Mohan, are you sure you can study as well as you did ten years ago?"

Without hesitation, I responded, "Yes. In fact, I'm confident I'll get even better grades now."

Mamatha smiled. "I'll support you no matter what you decide, Mohan."

Her words meant the world to me. The unwavering support of a spouse is invaluable, and for that, I was deeply grateful to Mamatha.

With her encouragement, I made the trip to the U.S. to visit institutions specializing in educating blind children and plan for Yogita's future. Financially, I was stretched thin, continually borrowing from private lenders to meet my commercial and personal needs.

Most of the schools I wanted to visit were on the West Coast, so I made appointments with two institutions in Los Angeles, sending them information and photos of Yogita beforehand. I booked a room in a hotel chain located downtown, close to the institutions.

When I arrived, though, I was stunned by the condition of the hotel. I had expected much more from a place in the U.S., but the reality was far different. The reception area was deserted when I arrived, and I had to wait twenty minutes before a staff member appeared to give me my key. The room itself was dirty, the bed uncomfortable, and the shower curtain repulsive. Still, I was so exhausted from the journey I collapsed into bed and slept deeply for twelve straight hours.

That night's rest was much-needed, but I couldn't help feeling a little disillusioned. This wasn't quite the America I had imagined.

The following day began with a beautiful sunny morning. After a quick breakfast of coffee from a flask at the reception, I set off for the Blind Children's Center. I stopped by a newspaper stand across the street, where an Indian man behind the counter kindly helped me with directions. "Two blocks this way, then take a right. It's the second or third building on your left. They have a big board. You can't miss it," he said, pointing in the direction.

The Blind Children's Center in Los Angeles was a nonprofit organization focused on empowering visually impaired children to live with their families in a sighted world. I was deeply impressed as I toured the center and saw the efforts to support these children through inclusive, family-centered early intervention and child development programs.

In India, schools for the blind were residential schools. Neither Mamatha or I understand how poverty or other compelling reasons could ever justify sending young blind children away from their families to these schools. We felt strongly that children, no matter their disabilities—whether blind, deaf, mute, paraplegic, or otherwise—deserved to stay with their families. Separating them, we thought, could never be the right solution. The Blind Children's Center was a beacon for families like mine.

I returned to the hotel, only to be greeted again by the unpleasant, musty smell of the lobby's neglected carpet and furniture. The tiny, rickety elevator was no better. As I squeezed in, I found myself face-to-face with three overly perfumed, underdressed escorts, their presence overwhelming in the small space. One of them blew smoke directly into my face as they made rude comments, making me even more uncomfortable.

Back in my room, I received a call from Azhar, my old college friend who had helped me set up my appointments. "Are you mad, Mona?" he scolded the moment I answered. "Why in the hell are you staying in a godforsaken downtown hotel in L.A.?"

I tried to explain, mumbling, "The special education center is just a block away."

"That's no excuse! Check out immediately and go to a decent hotel outside downtown," he commanded.

"It's already 7:00, Azhar," I reasoned. "I have an appointment at 9:30 tomorrow morning. I'll check out first thing after the meeting and find another place. Don't worry."

Azhar wasn't convinced, but I reassured him, promising to move to a better hotel.

The next morning, I headed to the Los Angeles Center for Special Education, a highly regarded facility specializing in early intervention speech and language therapy. Families from around the world sought out its quality services for their children. At the front desk, a young, stylish African American woman wearing large hoop earrings greeted me and led me into a meeting room.

The space was cozy, with a round table and four chairs. After sitting down to wait, I wandered over to the window, gazing at the downtown Los Angeles skyline. The sound of approaching footsteps, accompanied by the click of heels, prompted me to return to my seat.

A poised woman with auburn hair entered wearing a collared shirt and trousers. She smiled and introduced herself as she sat down next to me. "Hi, I'm Amy. You must be Mr. Ranga Ravo."

"Mohan Ranga Rao," I corrected with a smile as we shook hands.

"Must have been a long flight from India, Mr. Ravo."

"Please, call me Mohan. Yes, it was, but I'm doing fine."

"Mo-hann?" she repeated, drawing out the syllables carefully.

I nodded, thinking *Mo-Hann* was indeed much better than *Ravo.*

I shared Yogita's story and my plans for our family to move to the U.S. for her sake. I mentioned the residential schools in India I had heard about for blind girls. Amy immediately interrupted with a gentle shake of her head. "No, no, no. The idea of exclusive schools is pretty much outdated here, Mo-Hann. Nowadays, we include children with special needs in regular schools."

"So I'm learning. That's wonderful to hear," I replied.

"Decades ago, a blind school might have been the only option. But now, we send children to local schools, and the schools make the necessary accommodations."

I couldn't hide my excitement. "That's just great!"

"Yes. Many disabled people who went through what we now consider 'segregated' schools feel strongly about it. Words like 'integration' and 'inclusion' have taken on new significance," Amy explained.

I was genuinely moved by how far the system had come. "Wow."

"Yogita is still very young," Amy continued. "Right now, focus on teaching her self-help skills and making her as independent as possible. We'll take care of the rest once your family is in the U.S."

Amy's reassurance filled me with a sense of relief. Public perceptions in the U.S. had evolved in ways that made me feel confident this was the right place for Yogita. Before leaving, I collected some booklets on raising a child with visual impairment, feeling more sure about our decision to move.

After the positive meeting, I checked out of the downtown hotel and moved to the Hilton near Los Angeles Airport. Azhar joined me from Kansas the following morning, bursting into the room without even a greeting. "You need to settle down here with Mamatha and Yogita, Mona," he said, tossing his bag on the bed.

"Yes, Azhar, that is exactly what I intend to do," I replied, smiling at his straightforwardness. "How was the flight from Kansas?"

"Long enough to give me cramps," he said, rubbing his legs.

We spent some time catching up, reminiscing about our college days and old memories. He was shocked to hear about the family dispute, my struggles, and my eventual exit from the family business.

"I can't believe you brothers live separately now after spending nearly three decades together," he said, shaking his head in amazement.

Those memories seemed like a lifetime ago now. They were set in March 1982, when I was fresh out of post-graduation, and hedonistic adventures still dominated my personal life. Along with my friends, I indulged in a lifestyle that oscillated between jungle resorts and trips to Europe, checking bold items off my bucket list with a thrill that seemed to define my twenties.

Looking back, those years were marked by a constant balancing act—between proving myself in the family business and seeking personal excitement. It was a period when reckless abandon and responsibility collided, shaping my identity and ambitions.

Now, here I was, contemplating continuing my education from a completely different lens, with a wife and a blind daughter in tow.

I quickly shifted the conversation. "Anyway, let's talk about you. How's Sakina? How's Raza?" Sakina, his wife from Hyderabad, and their son, Raza, were frequent topics of our conversations.

"They're doing well," he said with a proud smile.

"Oh, by the way, I've stopped drinking," I told him, eager to share this personal victory.

Azhar looked at me approvingly. "That's the best thing you've done, Mona. How's Mamatha handling everything? It's always harder for the mother."

"She's holding up better than me, that's for sure."

Our conversation lingered on memories of home and what would be best for Yogita's future. As we wrapped up our visit, Azhar's words about the benefits of the U.S. deepened my sense of urgency about finding the best possible life for her. I would return to India with my sights set on America. *A home in a foreign country for my child.*

During the flight, I quickly calculated the commercial value of all my assets to determine how much I'd have left if I sold everything, paid off my debts, and relocated to the U.S. for Yogita's sake. The sum came to roughly 100,000 USD.

As soon as I landed, I went straight to the telephone booth and called Mamatha. "I just landed. How are you? How is Turry?"

"We're doing fine, Mona. Are you stopping over in Bangalore?" Mamatha asked.

"No, I'm eager to see Turry. I miss you both so much. I'll come straight to Mysore. I don't have time to visit your parents."

"Mohan, I have something to tell you."

A chill went down my spine. Flashes of Turry's struggles ran through my mind at lightning speed. "What is it, Mamatha?" I asked, my voice trembling with fear.

CHAPTER 13

Eyes Full of Promise

(1991 and 1992)

"I'm pregnant."

I was silent for what seemed like a full minute.

A strange mingling of fear and elation gripped my heart, making my mouth dry. I rolled my tongue over my parched lips. When I finally spoke, full of curiosity and apprehension, all I could say was, "Really?"

"Yes, Mona," Mamatha gleefully replied.

The seriousness of what was to come pressed down on me as I processed the news and forced myself to focus on the immediate task at hand. Not wanting to crush Mamatha's excitement, I took a deep breath and said, "I can't wait to talk more with you about such wonderful news! I'll see you and Turry soon."

I swiftly hailed a taxi outside Bangalore Airport's arrival gate. As I sank into the back seat, I closed my eyes with a flood of questions and fears racing through my mind: *Will this child be healthy? Will Mamatha face another threatened miscarriage? What if this baby also has disabilities? No*, I reassured myself. *The medical team at Pittsburgh Children's Hospital, along with the Mayo Clinic, confidently declared that Yogita's condition is a rare developmental anomaly. They assured us the chance of recurrence is almost nonexistent.*

As the taxi moved through the bustling city, the lights blurring past, I tried to find solace in this news. A healthy child could dispel the accusations from society—and even within myself—that I had somehow done something wrong. Mamatha and I would feel complete. But if not, it would confirm that our genes, not past sins, were the cause of Yogita's struggles.

This news meant I now had to rethink our plans for settling in the U.S.—whether I should abandon or postpone it for a few years. *What's the worst that could happen?* I reasoned. *Yogita could have another special child for company.* But I shook my head, recognizing my old habit of expecting the worst, trying to shield myself from disappointment before it even arrived.

I'm not going to let negative thoughts sabotage me.

Things will be fine.

I'll ensure my family is happy and keep dark forebodings out of my mind.

Yet, another fear lingered. Would our love for Yogita be divided once another child arrived? I thought about my own family—nine children, my parents always giving us their love without it feeling split. *Surely, our love would only multiply with another child, not diminish.* After all, Mamatha and I couldn't let Yogita's disabilities constrain our desire for more children.

Still, my mind raced through endless speculation.

Can Mamatha endure the nine months of pregnancy without constantly fearing that Yogita is the only type of child we can produce? Does she have the courage? I knew she did—her resolve was like a bull's. But fear doesn't always yield to logic.

I reminded myself that every pregnancy carries some risk. Our situation seemed more daunting only because we had already experienced it. But even if we did have another child with special needs, we were better prepared this time. More importantly, we loved Yogita fully and unconditionally—her disabilities were just one part of her identity. When I arrived home, I hugged Mamatha tight for what seemed like an eternity.

As the days went on, I continued to wrestle with my thoughts. Mamatha remained joyful, though cautious. She became meticulous about everything—what she ate, where she went, and even avoided medicine when sick, opting to ride out colds and fevers without intervention. When there was a lunar eclipse during the second month of her pregnancy, she locked herself in her room, following the old belief that eclipses could harm the baby. Week after week, we navigated our fears together, though Mamatha took on the role of the comforter more often than I did.

Our extended families, meanwhile, were unsure of how to help. Their silence only underscored how much Mamatha and I were on this journey alone, drawing strength from each other. As the weeks went by, we both felt the pressure of ensuring this child, unlike Yogita, would be born healthy—with full vision, free from any impairments. It was a heavy burden that we carried, but Mamatha, as always, bore the larger share. She was the one constantly reassuring me, even though I knew she struggled with her own fears.

Around her sixth week of pregnancy, Mamatha decided to consult Dr. Nirmala, a gynecologist renowned in our family. My six sisters-in-law had all gone to her, and she had a reputation for being gruff and tough yet incredibly wise—a giant of a woman with the heart of an angel.

"The first three to five months are extremely critical," Dr. Nirmala stated firmly during our first visit. "You have to see me every week. I'll order an ultrasound every month. Ultrasounds are safe."

Those months were arduous for Mamatha. On my part, I made sure she didn't lift anything heavy, especially Yogita. Mamatha attended to every small detail—meticulously following a diet plan and avoiding anything that could risk the pregnancy. She approached those first two trimesters with the same determination and care that had always defined her, sparing no effort to safeguard the health of our unborn child.

Every day, Mamatha drew courage and optimism from an inner reservoir that carried us through the uncertainty. We went for ultrasounds every month under the care of Dr. Rajeswar, a kind-hearted radiologist who happened to be my brother Sridhar's friend. He was one of those rare medical professionals who took extra care to put his patients at ease before sharing results. During one of the scans, he pointed out the eye sockets. "They are clearly visible and well-developed," he said. "I'm very confident the baby's eye formation is perfect. She's a very healthy baby girl."

"Isn't that wonderful, Mona? A healthy girl!" Mamatha's excitement was infectious.

While she brightened with joy after each scan, visibly uplifted by the numerous images of our developing daughter, I quietly wrestled with anxiety. The memories of Yogita's birth and the shock of her blindness haunted me, lurking in the back of my mind despite the doctor's reassurances. Yet, I hid these fears, not wanting to cast a shadow over Mamatha's courage.

In the seventh month, Mamatha's anxieties surfaced whenever the baby didn't kick for a few hours. She panicked, her face tight with worry, until another ultrasound showed everything was normal.

Our day of reckoning arrived once more on November 8, 1991. It was a Friday, and Mamatha was nearing full term. She had been complaining of persistent back pain, and though I was reluctant to leave her alone, I went to the office, knowing she would have her hands full managing both Yogita and the approaching labor. I still remember the call I received around noon.

"Mohan, please come at once. I think my water just broke."

I sped in my Jeep to pick her up, then headed straight to Aditya Hospital, a short distance from our home in Gokulam. After swiftly filling out the registration form, I accompanied Mamatha to the maternity section and, with the nurse, helped her settle into a room.

By 7 p.m., Mamatha's contractions had intensified, and the delivery team brought her into the labor ward. I waited outside, my nerves taut with tension and an intense fear concerning the health of our baby's eyes. The soft, hushed footsteps of the nurses and the distant hum of medical equipment seemed to heighten my anxious anticipation and dread.

Time felt suspended, with each second dragging as my watch ticked steadily, indifferent to the turmoil inside me. Two hours crawled by, and I was pacing outside the labor ward, my anxiety growing with every step, unable to find any semblance of calm.

Finally, a nurse emerged and, in a calm tone, informed me, "It's a girl."

My heart raced with desperation. "Are her eyes okay?" I asked urgently.

The nurse nodded, but her gaze fell away from mine, leaving me more apprehensive.

Is she being diplomatic? Is she hiding something? My fear spiked as I rushed into the labor ward, desperate for clarity.

Our second child, Rachita, was born at 9:12 p.m. in Mysore. Both Mamatha and I instantly recognized, the moment we laid eyes on our newborn, that she had eyes full of promise. She could see. That moment is forever etched in my memory, a precious memory I will cherish for the rest of my life. The contrast was striking between eyes that could see and eyes that could not. Yogita had barely opened her eyes during the first few days of her life. Yet, on day one, Rachita's eyes were wide open and brimming with life. Her jet-black irises, set against the white sclera, were like morning dew to our parched souls.

Guru came to see the baby, and when I told him Rachita's eyes were normal and healthy, he asked, "How can you tell?"

His question initially irritated me, but I was working on overcoming my sensitivity. I reminded myself that he didn't intend to offend or upset me with his inquiry. "I just know, Guru," I replied.

My mother-in-law arrived promptly with Yogita. Seeing her little face lighting up at my voice and how she eagerly grasped my finger after being apart nearly nine hours warmed my heart. Compared to the tiny, delicate newborn, Yogita seemed so grown up, no longer a baby herself.

My father-in-law visited from Bangalore, overjoyed with the arrival of our healthy baby. "Mohan, congratulations. You now have three kids to look after," he said, grinning.

I smiled in response. He had once told me, a few weeks after my marriage, that Mamatha was like an innocent child due to the protective way he had raised her, always hovering over her.

Yogita, at two-and-a-half years old, was about to face a significant change with the arrival of her new sister. Mamatha and I were both eager and anxious to see how she would adjust to this new addition to our family.

When we brought Rachita home on the first day, Mamatha and I placed Yogita and Rachita between us on our bed, watching their interaction closely. Initially, Yogita seemed fascinated by Rachita's cooing and wailing, her mouth agape with curiosity. She made no attempt to reach out and touch her sister.

It wasn't until we guided Yogita's hand to Rachita's hair and face that she began exploring her sister, gently moving her fingers over Rachita's tiny body. Throughout this exploration, Yogita never pulled Rachita's hair or touched her with any intent to harm. It was a heartening start to what we hoped would be a loving relationship between the two siblings.

Rachita's arrival was nothing short of a divine blessing. Her eyes, even at just a week old, were lively and responsive, capturing our gaze and filling our hearts with joy. While a wave of pity for Yogita would occasionally wash over us, our relief and happiness at Rachita's perfect health quickly replaced it.

By three weeks, Rachita would gaze at me intently whenever I brought my face close to hers. By the time she was two months old, she had developed a steady head. At three and a half months, she started swiping at dangling toys and shaking hand toys with growing curiosity. The greatest delight came when she began smiling and sticking out her tongue in response to mine, even though she was barely three months old. By six months, Rachita responded to her name and babbled consonants, bringing a new dynamic into our home.

During those six months, Yogita's sleeping habits began to normalize. Rachita's frequent cries kept Yogita awake during the day, creating a new routine in our household. As a parent, I felt immense joy at Rachita's milestones. Yet, every joy was tinged with a shadow of sadness, wondering why God had not granted Yogita the same normalcy.

One particular Sunday afternoon, while we were watching Rachita and Yogita lying side by side, with Rachita sucking on her bottle and Yogita gently feeling her sister's hair, Mamatha pondered, "Mohan, why don't we fully appreciate the countless organs and senses we have given to us so unconditionally and in such perfect health?"

I was also thinking about it at that moment, so it was like she was reading my mind. "I know," I replied. "We often take our senses for granted, only missing them or wishing for them when someone we love is deprived. But look at how happy Yogita seems. In a way, she is blessed because she remains unaware of her condition."

"So true," Mamatha replied.

Later that day, I sat on the entrance ramp of our house, strumming my guitar and humming the Eagles' "Best of My Love." I hoped Yogita would come and sit next to me as she usually did, her face lighting up with excitement as I played her favorite songs. For me, entertaining Yogita was more than just playing music. I cherished the moments when I could see her reactions, the joy she derived from the simple pleasure of my guitar and voice. Her facial expressions, clapping, and enthusiastic gestures revealed how deeply she felt joy just like any other child.

As the rain poured down outside, I continued to strum and sing, but Yogita did not appear.

"Mohan, come and see this!" Mamatha called from inside, her laughter ringing out.

"What is it?" I yelled, pulling my fingers from the strings.

"Come and see for yourself," she said, still laughing.

Curious, I went inside to find Yogita lying on the mat, happily sucking on Rachita's feeding bottle. Rachita, meanwhile, was lying on her tummy, joyfully observing her older sister and giggling. The sight was heartwarming and hilarious, a delightful snapshot of our growing family dynamics.

Such moments were a reminder of how quickly time was passing. At eleven months, Rachita took her first steps, and toward the end of Rachita's first year, Yogita began to realize the differences between herself and her younger sister. I noticed the look of longing on Yogita's face when she heard Rachita babbling and saw her subtle attempts to mimic her sister. She understood she should also be able to do that, but couldn't.

Even though it felt like Rachita had just arrived, she was already leaving her mark on our lives, drawing Yogita into her world in the most innocent and endearing ways. Day by day, their bond deepened.

By the time Rachita turned one, she was playing with Yogita. Rachita would hold Yogita's hand and guide her on short walks, and she delighted in feeding Yogita bananas or her favorite ice cream, treating her like a live Barbie doll. Yogita, in turn, developed a deep affection for Rachita. Her sister's constant presence became a source of comfort, and she would become restless if Rachita was absent for too long.

As Rachita's bond with Yogita deepened, her instinct to protect her sister became more evident. Whether at a bustling restaurant or a crowded family gathering, Rachita was always by Yogita's side, guiding her with a tenderness reflecting the purity of childhood. It was a reminder of the innocence many cultures, including our own, revere as a reflection of divinity. Yet, even as we marveled at their connection, we knew the complexities of life would soon begin to shape them as the world inevitably introduces the illusion of self, or *maya*, as described in Hindu scriptures.

These reflections often led Mamatha and me to contemplate what the future might hold for our family. One evening, while folding towels in our bedroom, Mamatha calmly yet thoughtfully asked a question that had been weighing on her mind for some time. "Mohan, do you think we should have another child?"

"No way," I immediately replied. I didn't want to be insensitive, but it was my knee-jerk reaction. "It would be best if you didn't undergo another nerve-wracking pregnancy. Besides, I'm thirty-four. I'm not interested in having more children."

Mamatha didn't respond immediately, her expression remained indifferent, as though she was already weighing our family's future beyond this conversation. As she folded the last of the towels, she shifted to Yogita's needs and what would be best for her as she continued to develop. "Mohan, I don't think moving to the U.S. is a good idea anymore. Yogita seems very happy and settled. I'm happy, too. Your extended family is here, and my parents are close by. My mom is really very helpful. What do you think?"

In the previous year, we had ruled out the idea of enrolling Yogita in a specialized school. Instead, we wanted to explore options like homeschooling or attending a regular school with an attendant's support.

"I think I should focus on making enough money for us to visit the U.S. every year and stay updated on the latest developments regarding special needs," I suggested.

"That makes sense. I like that," Mamatha agreed.

And with that, we quietly let go of the idea of moving to the U.S. for good.

CHAPTER 14

Light at the End of the Tunnel

(1993 - 1995)

Watching Yogita and Rachita grow and play together over the next few years was pure joy. The beauty of children lies in their innocent disregard for differences, whether trivial or profound. Unaware of Yogita's limitations, Rachita played with her sister as though nothing separated them. It was as if God had intertwined their lives with a gentle hand, each moment reflecting the beauty of unconditional love, untouched by Yogita's inability to reciprocate fully.

While the girls' bond offered me solace, the reality in my business world was far more complex. I knew I was standing at a critical juncture. Six years had passed since I severed ties with my family's company, driven by the need to prove myself independently, but the last four years had been a brutal teacher. Desperate for financial relief, I turned to everyone I could think of—my auditor, business vendors, customers, friends—silence. Even my brothers were more concerned about their financial guarantees for my loans than offering any support.

I had invested heavily in tetramisole, which was still idle due to the Chinese market dumping—this left machinery and over fifty workers without purpose. My food company barely broke even, forcing me to seek a corporate partner to save Arvee.

Thankfully, a meeting with a potential partner led to a job-work arrangement, starting with propyl-theophylline conversion, which gradually utilized our capacity and revived our business, trickling in some cash flow to keep us going.

Noticing an idle autoclave at their facility, I negotiated its purchase despite financial strain and warnings about its risks. Borrowing at steep interest, I ventured into high-pressure hydrogenation, defying doubts. Within a year, the autoclave transformed Arvee, enabling large-scale hydrogenation and earning recognition for innovation in noble metal catalyst reductions.

The stress from the business upheavals of the past began to ease, and this newfound tranquility mirrored the peace and joy I was experiencing with my family. Mamatha and I took more weekend vacations and started to socialize more with my extended family, relishing the time we spent together.

Mamatha, content with her role of caring for the kids, kept busy while I continued to pour my energy into working sixty hours a week, breathing new life into both of my businesses. Still, we managed to carve out time for ourselves—going for evening drives twice a week and enjoying short family picnics on the weekends.

Every Sunday, the four of us would go on long drives with the music turned up, which Yogita loved. One song in particular, "Ironic" by Alanis Morissette, became her favorite. She especially enjoyed the pauses in the song, where Alanis would suddenly belt out the next line. As soon as the music resumed after a pause, Yogita would break into uncontrollable giggles, and Mamatha, Rachita, and I couldn't help but laugh along with her.

By then, Yogita had grown older and was more manageable. She had developed her own way of communicating—she made a hissing sound when she needed to go to the toilet, when she was hungry, or even when she was bored. Rachita, always eager to help, would keep Yogita company, give her baths, and take her around the house. Despite being six, however, Yogita still hadn't spoken a word. She relied entirely on her hissing sounds to express herself.

Dealing with the realities of Yogita's condition paled in comparison to the insensitivity we still encountered occasionally. Without knowing her story, strangers would assume Yogita was an underdeveloped child. This happened often at restaurants, where people would cast judgmental glances or make quiet remarks.

Eventually, I came to realize these people didn't see what we saw and needed more context for how Mamatha and I lived every day. I would remind myself that Yogita is who she is because she is meant to be who she is. It's part of the Universe's plan, which is why she exists as she does in the world. It's as simple as that. Often in life, you don't get what you expect, but the Universe has a way of making you love what you have. Because of Yogita, I feel so much gratitude and love. My eyeless angel became my eye-opener.

Yogita's presence in my life changed the way I saw everything, especially my expectations and my perspective on happiness. Her role made me more sensitive and less judgmental. She strengthened our family's bond and deepened the love we shared. Because of Yogita, I learned to give others the benefit of the doubt. Before she came into my life, I used to make snap judgments when I saw a child having a meltdown in a grocery store or crying in a movie theater, thinking it was just a *bratty kid* or *bad parenting*. But now, I understand that everyone has their own story, and things aren't always as they seem.

As for Rachita, she was a whirlwind of energy, constantly moving and full of life. We affectionately called her "Tornado" because she would take over any room she entered, creating a storm of activity. Yogita had grown used to her noisy presence, and over time, it became clear she even missed Rachita when she wasn't around. Whenever Rachita was away, Yogita would become restless, and that restlessness would melt away in a flash when her sister returned home. Their bond, though unspoken, was undeniable.

Yogita's blindness, once a source of constant worry, began to fade from our focus. We no longer saw her through the lens of her limitations. Instead, we saw her as herself: a joyful, radiant child. In that newfound clarity, I found myself growing emotionally and spiritually, embracing both of my daughters for the light they brought into our lives.

A reflection of my home life, my business's growing success was also bringing a sense of stability and accomplishment. At last, the light at the end of the tunnel wasn't just a distant hope. With the financial stress subsided, we focused on creating more lasting family memories. It was the perfect time to plan something special—a break from the day-to-day grind and a chance to focus on each other.

In early 1994, the excitement of our planned month-long trip to the U.S. filled our house. Mamatha meticulously packed, organizing everything for our daughters. As I double-checked the tickets and travel documents, the girls seemed especially giddy, like they could sense something special was coming. The anticipation was palpable for our first big family vacation.

The flight to America felt like an eternity, especially with two young children. Rachita, barely four years old, bounced with energy while Yogita sat anxiously beside her, curious about her enthusiasm. "Are we almost there, Appa?" Rachita asked every half hour, her excitement barely contained. Yogita smiled hearing her sister's voice, even if the concept of distance was still vague to her. "Almost, Kanna," I replied, glancing at Mamatha, who gave me a reassuring smile.

After a few days in Washington, D.C., exploring the monuments and indulging in museum visits, we made our way to Florida. Disney World was the highlight of the trip, especially for the girls. The joy in Rachita's face was only rivaled by the wonder in Yogita's. Though Yogita couldn't see the dazzling lights or the colorful characters, she felt the magic in the air. Rachita, ever the little caretaker, was glued to her sister's side, holding her hand at every turn.

"I want to sit with Yogita, Amma!" Rachita squealed as we stood in line for a ride.

"Are you sure? It might be too fast for her," Mamatha cautioned.

But Yogita seemed ready for the adventure, already bouncing on her toes.

"Let her try, Amma," I chimed in, adjusting my camera, ready to capture the moment.

The roller coaster whipped us around the track, and despite the high-pitched screams from the other children on the ride, Yogita let out the loudest squeal of delight. Her laughter echoed through the air, hands raised to her face as the wind rushed past her. Rachita, beside her, clung to her seat with wide eyes, laughing between shrieks. "Again! Again!" she insisted as soon as the ride ended, her face glowing with exhilaration.

By the end of our week in Florida, we were all exhausted but happy. The girls slept soundly, their dreams no doubt filled with roller coasters, talking animals, and joyous laughter. Mamatha and I sat on the hotel balcony, looking at the moonlit sky.

"Can you believe how much Rachita looks after Yogita? She's so protective," Mamatha said softly, her eyes filled with pride.

I nodded. "They have a special bond," I replied, wrapping my arm around her shoulders. "It's like Rachita senses what Yogita needs, even without her saying a word."

The rest of the trip took us to Chicago, where we explored the bustling city streets and went to specialized centers where therapists confirmed we were on the right track with Yogita's speech and cognitive therapies. That reassurance lifted a weight off our shoulders. Each visit to those centers strengthened our resolve to continue giving her the best possible care.

After returning home, life slipped back into its familiar rhythm. Mamatha, who had learned to drive just a few years earlier when

Rachita was a baby, now had her own car—a silver sedan I had given her. The freedom gave her a new sense of independence, and soon enough, she was often taking the girls to parks and gardens.

One breezy afternoon, I arrived home to the sight of Mamatha pulling into the driveway, Yogita's laughter echoing from the back seat.

Rachita jumped out first and ran to me, her little legs barely able to contain her energy. "Appa! We saw ducks! And Amma let us feed them bread!" she shouted excitedly.

Yogita followed, carefully stepping out of the car with a serene smile.

Mamatha, though tired as the main caretaker, had the same glow I had seen throughout our recent trip to the U.S. Despite the challenges, she was the anchor for our family, the one who made sure both girls thrived, although that was a lot more work for her because of Yogita's needs. "You should have been there, Mohan," Mamatha said, shaking her head with a smile. "Yogita didn't want to leave the park. She was running her hands over the flowers, feeling the petals. Rachita was guiding her the whole time." Her eyes softened as she spoke, and I could see her pride and love for our daughters.

As much as I helped after work, Mamatha bore the most responsibility of daily life. Thankfully, around that time, my administrative manager at P&N Foods, Manoj Mammen, took on additional responsibility as my executive assistant. He kindly offered to ask his mother, Susan, a retired kindergarten teacher, if she would consider becoming a governess for Yogita. I accepted his offer gratefully, and soon, Susan became part of our family.

In her late forties and small in stature, Susan was a strong woman in every sense. The moment she met Yogita, she developed a deep affection for her. Yogita, too, felt at ease with Susan right from the start.

With Susan's help, Mamatha could spend more time with Rachita, whose needs were vastly different from Yogita's. Every morning, Susan would take Yogita to a nearby park, where large cement molds of various animals fascinated her. Yogita loved exploring their textures, running her hands over the contours while hearing birds chirping and children laughing. As Susan cared for Yogita, life settled into a new rhythm. Rachita, always nearby, filled the house with her endless questions, while Yogita spent her peaceful mornings under Susan's attentive care.

Susan's dedication to Yogita was remarkable. She protected her with quiet devotion, reminding us of the bond between Anne Sullivan and Helen Keller. However, Susan's nurturing was softer and more grandmotherly. Her gentle approach brought much-needed relief to Mamatha, allowing her to focus more easily on each daughter.

As our family continued to evolve in its new rhythm, the park in front of our home in Gokulam started attracting an unsavory kind of attention. Vagabonds began gathering there, creating an uneasy atmosphere—especially for Mamatha when I was away. Sensing the growing discomfort, I knew it was time to find a new home where our family could feel secure again.

It had been six years since we married, so it was definitely time to own our home. While many vacant lots were available, constructing a house would be time-consuming and costly. Instead, I looked for houses that were ready for immediate move-in. During one of my searches, I found a fully constructed house in Jayalakshmi Puram, situated on a 5,800-square-foot lot. It was well-planned, near a temple, and ideal for a nuclear family, with three bedrooms. The owner had relocated to Singapore, and I managed to negotiate a final price of Rs. 2.7 million.

In keeping with Hindu tradition, we named our new home "Sitara"—a name that incorporated the first two syllables of my mother's name, Sita, and the first two letters of my father's name, Ranga.

We moved into Sitara on July 19, 1994.

After transferring all our belongings, I made one last visit to our Gokulam house. I inspected the kitchen, the front bedroom, and the living room before finally entering our master bedroom.

The sight of the large teak wood bed with rosewood backrest that we left behind, where Mamatha and I had slept with Rachita next to me and Yogita next to Mamatha, triggered a wave of nostalgia. I suddenly remembered the times Yogita would get off the bed, circle the bed, and pull on my hand to join her. The bathroom door, ajar, brought back memories of Yogita's favorite pastime—opening the tap in the middle of the night. Or her favorite prank of all, to turn on the air conditioning while we all slept!

As I stood there, a deep sense of sorrow enveloped me, and I broke down, sobbing uncontrollably. The memories were bittersweet, and the realization we were leaving behind so much of our past was overwhelming. It felt as though we had been carried on a relentless tide, reminding me that life, despite its hardships, keeps moving forward.

Later that year, as we settled into our new home, Mamatha and I decided to celebrate our wedding anniversary. We took Yogita and Rachita to Goa and stayed at The Leela Resorts again. This time, the air felt lighter—no French couple swearing at us from the adjoining room, just the sound of the ocean's soothing waves.

A couple of months after returning home from that wonderful trip, Mamatha called me at the office with a request that caught me off guard.

"Mohan, can you stop by a medical store and pick up one of those imported pregnancy test kits on your way home?" Her voice was calm with an undercurrent of anxiety.

"Why?" I asked, confused. *I thought we agreed on no more children?*

"I missed my period," she replied simply.

I quickly went to the store and grabbed two different types of pregnancy tests. When I got home, I handed them to Mamatha, who took them and headed to the bathroom.

After a few tense minutes, she emerged, holding one of the tests. "This color is pink, right?" she asked, her eyes searching mine for confirmation.

I nodded, my heart pounding.

CHAPTER 15

Light Eclipsed by Darkness

(1996 and 1997)

I felt kicked in the gut.

I was terrified of taking another chance. I didn't want Mamatha to endure another nine months of hardship. I lacked her immense courage.

"How on earth did you manage this, Mamatha? Are you sure it's from me?" I demanded, glaring at her.

Mamatha met my gaze defiantly, winning the "who blinks first" contest. "Remember our Goa trip in July?" she asked with a hint of mischief, turning away coyly.

What began as a moment of lightheartedness quickly gave way to weeks of anxiety. As the pregnancy progressed, a deepening sense of concern overshadowed the memories of the playful night in Goa.

Leela, Mamatha's mother, arrived in Mysore in January 1996. Her support was invaluable to Mamatha. It was a special occasion for Leela to join our family in celebrating Mamatha's birthday on the 7th of February. Rachita was particularly fond of Leela, whom she affectionately called "Ajji." While Yogita loved her just as much, she was never able to say it.

Rachita would often stroke Mamatha's tummy and ask repeatedly, "When will the baby come out?"

"Soon," she would always respond with a gentle smile, resting her hand on her belly as if already cradling the new life within.

On the morning of March 25, 1996, that "soon" came suddenly. Thankfully, I was home that day, and we were sitting in the living room when Mamatha gasped, her hand flying to her stomach. "Mona, it's time," she said, her voice a mix of urgency and calm. Her water had broken, and within seconds, I grabbed the hospital bag we had prepared weeks earlier, ushering her out the door. Her mother and Susan were already at our home, anticipating this moment.

The hospital was just down the road, but the drive felt like an eternity. My heart raced as I kept glancing at Mamatha, breathing steadily beside me, her fingers clenched tightly around the edge of her seat. We were at the hospital within minutes, and the nurses, sensing the urgency, quickly ushered her into the delivery room.

I paced the sterile, white-tiled hallway, my mind running through every possible scenario, a thousand silent prayers tumbling out with each step. Finally, after what felt like hours, a newborn's cry pierced the air. I rushed to the delivery room, my pulse quickening.

There, lying in Mamatha's arms, was our son, his eyes wide and curious, blinking in the fluorescent hospital lights. The moment I saw his eyes, an overwhelming wave of relief swept over me. "He can see," I whispered, my voice barely audible, but Mamatha understood. We exchanged looks of immense gratitude and unspoken relief as I stroked her hair from her forehead for the third time.

Mamatha's mother, who had been waiting anxiously outside, burst into the room, her face flushed with excitement. "Another grandchild!" she exclaimed, her voice brimming with joy.

I leaned over Mamatha, my heart full. She looked exhausted and radiant, her face soft with that post-birth glow. "Thank you, Mamatha," I whispered.

She smiled up at me, her eyes brimming with a silent understanding of all we had gone through to arrive at this moment.

As I gazed at my son—with his small, perfect features and the light in his eyes—I realized how grateful I was for Mamatha's insistence on having another child. We named him Rahul, and our family was now complete.

Dr. Nirmala, our gynecologist, and Dr. Rajeswar, our trusted radiologist and friend, had been on high alert for the whole pregnancy. Only after our baby boy was born healthy did they finally confess how nervous they had been all along.

Ever unpredictable, the world does not pause for moments of joy. As with all things in life, we cannot avoid adversity, no matter how much we wish we could.

As we grow older and gain more experience, overcoming past hurdles should give us the wisdom to navigate new challenges as they arise. However, that doesn't necessarily make them any easier.

About a year after Rahul was born, Rachita was six, and Yogita had just turned eight. Soon after Mamatha went to check on the kids, who should have been sleeping, she quickly returned to our room in distress, crying uncontrollably. "Mona! I found Yogita playing with her private parts! She is only eight. What will happen when she grows up?"

I did my best not to sound concerned. We were parents of young children, and perhaps this was something we could expect as they grow and explore. "Come on, Mamatha. Masturbation is not such a big deal. Turry must have discovered it by accident."

"No, Mona. It's sudden. I keep a watch on Turry twenty-four-seven. I do not think she learned it by herself."

We fell silent.

Mamatha calmed down and suddenly appeared lost in thought. "Mona," Mamatha said, raising her voice, "Dr. Ramya is the only one who touches Yogita, and Susan is there for the full four hours from eight to noon."

Dr. Ramya was the clinical psychologist conducting daily sessions for Yogita's cognitive development.

"You know what? Susan told me recently that Dr. Ramya keeps Yogita in her office and locks the door from the inside for more than an hour. Ramya must be touching Yogita inappropriately when she is alone with her," she declared.

"What?" I was shocked and horrified. "Why didn't you tell me this before?"

"She told me just the day before yesterday."

"We will stop sending Yogita. I will talk to Dr. Budhisagar," I said, not even considering alternatives.

Mamatha exclaimed, "We cannot get her married, and with the beauty she possesses, she will be unsafe in this cruel world when she grows up." Mamatha choked back her tears.

At that point, all I could think about was what kind of business Ramya could possibly have with Yogita alone, behind locked doors? I could feel my blood pressure rise.

"If Yogita's counselor herself abuses her, what chance does Yogita have after we die, Mona?" Mamatha started sobbing again. In agony, she blurted out, "I pray to God to take Yogita away from any of that!"

We stopped sending Yogita to Dr. Ramya from that day on and decided to identify an alternate place for her cognitive training. I also approached the educational board to file a formal complaint against Dr. Ramya to shield others from potential harm.

My biggest frustration for Yogita was not that she was blind but that she could not speak to tell us what was happening. It was the most heartbreaking aspect of her disability at that point. Although we could understand each other for the basics, so much was left unsaid and not understood.

Soon after this occurrence, in early July 1997, on our ninth wedding anniversary, Yogita developed a viral fever, which recurred twice in August. Until then, she had been a remarkably healthy girl, rarely catching so much as a cold in her eight years. By the end of August, we noticed unusual swelling below both of her earlobes and decided to take her to see Dr. Prashanth.

After carefully examining the swollen lymph nodes, he said, "I'd like to run a few routine blood tests on her. Please take her to Bhagavan Pathology Lab for these tests."

That same evening, Mamatha and I took Yogita to the lab, where they drew her blood sample. They asked us to return for the results the next day, despite it being Ganesh Chaturthi, a major festival.

The next morning, I sat with Mamatha at our small kitchen dinette, sipping coffee and glancing at the headlines of the *Sunday Times*.

Mamatha suddenly said with a spark of excitement, "Mohan, in all our nine years of marriage, you've never performed *Ganesh Puja* at home. Why don't you do it today? I even bought a cassette that narrates every step of the ritual, along with the chants."

I lowered my reading glasses and gave her a skeptical look, wondering if she was serious. "Mamatha, I've told you after all our experiences with shamans, rituals, and pilgrimages—I don't believe in prayers or worship anymore," I said, my voice heavy with reluctance.

"Mohan, please, just this once, for my sake," she pleaded, her eyes reflecting a quiet desperation.

Though I believed God was beyond appeasement through worship, Mamatha's eagerness and pleading eyes persuaded me to give in and perform the Puja. I donned my holy thread, retrieved the *dhoti* I had tucked away in the corner of my wardrobe, and, precisely at 8 a.m., went to our Puja room (a small prayer room in our home).

Mamatha had already prepared the space with meticulous care, setting Lord Ganesha on a bed of shimmering rice grains and adorning the idol with vibrant marigolds and the delicate *Gejje Vastra*, a symbolic cotton ornament. The air was fragrant with the scent of sandalwood and jasmine. She gently guided Yogita and Rachita to sit beside her, their small forms leaning contently against the wall. Rahul, restless but curious, nestled into my lap. Yogita's face was calm as she listened to the rhythmic chanting from the tape recorder, her hands absently feeling the folds of her dress, while Rachita watched with wide-eyed curiosity.

Our Puja room was small and sacred, a tranquil cubicle with smooth marble floors that reflected the soft glow of the oil lamp. The marble-tiled walls gleamed in the dim light, surrounding a raised platform where Mamatha had thoughtfully arranged the idols—Lords Krishna, Shiva, Vishnu, and Ganesha. Each deity stood tall, garlanded with flowers and offerings, their serene faces bathed in the warm light.

I began the ritual by lighting a lamp filled with gingelly oil, the tiny flame flickering in the still air. As I poured holy water over the Ganesha idol for the *Abhishekam* (purification), the cool liquid ran down the smooth contours of the deity, glistening under the light. I chanted along with the mantras from the cassette, my voice faltering but earnest, following the priest's rhythmic voice wherever I could keep up.

The room filled with the sacred sounds of the bell as the Puja neared its end. I offered handfuls of fragrant flowers at the base of the Ganesha idol, their soft petals landing with reverence. Mamatha, her face glowing with quiet joy, turned to Yogita and Rachita, gently guiding their little palms together in a reverent namaste. Yogita's hands moved slightly as if sensing the seriousness of the moment, while Rachita eagerly mimicked her mother's gesture. I helped Rahul bring his tiny, pudgy hands together, his giggles breaking the quiet solemnity of the ritual.

For the first time in my thirty-nine years, I prayed with all my heart. Each word I uttered was imbued with the full spectrum of my worries and hopes, particularly after Yogita's recent struggles with her fevers. I performed the Puja with more devotion than I had ever imagined possible, carefully following the cassette priest's guidance as if it were a lifeline. The ritual lasted about forty-five minutes, yet time seemed to stand still in that sacred space.

As the final chants echoed and the bell rang once more, Mamatha's eyes glistened with satisfaction. She was overjoyed, her heart brimming with the hope that this collective act of devotion would bring prosperity, healing, and happiness to our family.

At 12:30 p.m., we made our way back to the clinic in our new Ford Escort. I put Yogita's favorite Fleetwood Mac CD on the car stereo, my heart pounding with an unease I couldn't quite shake despite the beautiful ritual I had just performed. When we arrived, I parked on the street across from the clinic, leaving Mamatha and the children in the car to wait for me.

The walls seemed to close in on me while I approached the counter alone to collect Yogita's report. The lobby was eerily quiet, and the receptionist was nowhere in sight. I shifted nervously from one foot to the other, the silence amplifying my anxiety.

After what felt like an eternity, the receptionist reappeared, her expression professional and distant. "Sir, Dr. Bhagavan would like to speak with you. Please go inside."

My hands trembled slightly as I followed her instructions. The thought of speaking directly with a pathologist was unsettling; it was an unusual practice, and the critical nature of the situation was not lost on me. I pushed open the door to the consultation room and stepped inside.

Dr. Bhagavan sat behind his desk, a compact figure with a fair complexion and an authoritative air that permeated the room. With his gaze locked on a report in his hands, he motioned for me to sit. "I need to speak with Dr. Prashanth urgently," he said, still studying the report. "I've tried his number, but he isn't answering."

I sat down, a sense of unease growing as I waited for him to address me directly.

"Who is this girl, Yogita?" he asked, finally setting the report aside and looking at me directly.

"She is my daughter," I replied, my voice trembling. "Why? Is there something wrong, Doctor?"

"Have you come alone?"

"No. My family is waiting in the car. I'm Dr. Sridhar's brother. What's the matter?"

"Oh, I know Sridhar well," Dr. Bhagavan said, nodding. "I'll call him and send him the report." He requested his number.

"223507," I replied, my anxiety mounting with each passing moment.

"Please wait outside," he instructed, preparing to make the call.

My legs felt weak as I rose from the chair, a sudden surge of overwhelming panic engulfing every inch of my body like a searing flame. "Please tell me, Doctor, is there any issue with her?" I pleaded.

He was silent for a few seconds. "You know I'm not allowed to explain this report to you. Your doctor or brother needs to do that."

"Please, Doctor. She's been blind since birth. We've already been through quite a lot with her," I said, looking for some sympathy.

He took a moment to reconsider, and while avoiding my gaze, he said, "There is a significant problem."

"Why? What is it? What's wrong with her?" My voice cracked as I choked back tears.

"She has a very advanced form of leukemia."

The words felt distant, almost inaudible. I froze, standing helplessly facing the desk, even as Dr. Bhagavan continued speaking.

"It's reached stage four. I'll call your brother so he can explain things further to you."

I stumbled out of the doctor's office and grasped the reception table for support. A few moments later, I left the lab without even asking for the report.

Each step toward the exit felt like a step into an abyss. When I finally reached the clinic's entrance, I stood with tears streaming down my cheeks, looking across the street at my family in our parked car. I saw Yogita sitting in the backseat, her feet up, beside Rachita. Even from where I stood, I could hear the music playing. Mamatha was in the front passenger seat with Rahul on her lap, clapping his tiny hands to the beat of the music.

With slow, deliberate steps, I crossed the road, took the driver's seat, and fastened my seatbelt. I didn't turn down the volume or say a word.

After a few moments, Mamatha's intuition pierced through the silence. She turned to me, eyes wide and probing, searching for answers in my tear-streaked face. "What is it, Mohan? Where is the report?" Her voice trembled, laced with anxiety, then her expression crumpled with dread. "Tell me, tell me!" she cried out, her voice a raw, jagged edge of fear as she reached to switch off the music.

The sudden silence was deafening.

Barely above a whisper, dragging the words out of me, each heavier than the last, I relayed the crushing news.

Mamatha's reaction was visceral. She began shaking her head with an intensity that seemed to challenge reality itself, as if by denying it, she could somehow alter our fate. Her distress rapidly escalated into hysteria, and despite my own overwhelming grief, I needed to calm her. The fear of frightening the two children in the backseat gripped me tightly.

"Appa, why is Amma crying?" Rachita's innocent question cut through the chaos, her wide eyes reflecting confusion.

Rahul, oblivious to the magnitude of the situation, tugged persistently at Mamatha's skirt, seeking her attention. All the while,

Yogita remained engrossed in the simple pleasure of playing with an empty cassette cover, her world seemingly untouched by the turmoil around her.

Remembering the music, I turned it back on, cranking up the volume to drown out the tears and tension as I drove us straight to Sridhar's house. When we arrived, Rachita darted out of the car with gleeful energy, her delighted squeals echoing across the yard as she spotted her cousin Nikhil, Sridhar's eight-year-old son.

We entered the house and saw Sridhar still engaged in a call on the landline extension phone. He was dressed in formal attire that seemed almost out of place in the somber moment. Deep fatigue replaced his usual composure. As he finally hung up, he sighed heavily and stood up to embrace me. I had never seen him so profoundly sad in the thirty-nine years I had known him.

"Mona. I'm so sorry, brother. Yogita's cancer is acute and very rare. She has lymphoblastoid leukemia. It progresses very rapidly," Sridhar said, his voice breaking and trailing off. He composed himself and continued. "I suppose God could no longer bear to see such an innocent and pure soul in this cruel world, and it's only God's will that she should not suffer more."

"I don't understand, Sri. Why would God single out one little girl and burden her with such terrible suffering?"

"I guess there is a larger purpose that only time will reveal."

"That sounds too cliched, Sri," I said, a snort of grief escaping me. Sridhar remained silent.

"What now, Sri?" I asked, blowing my nose. "Should I take her to Bharat Cancer Hospital? They say it's the best in Mysore."

"Mona, acute leukemia progresses very rapidly. We can put her on chemotherapy, but I do not recommend it since Yogita cannot express her distress," Sridhar said in a deep and sorrowful voice. "It's a decision you and Mamatha must make."

Mamatha broke down, and I struggled to keep my tears at bay, swallowing hard.

Sridhar squeezed my shoulder in silent support.

We returned home with the weightiest ethical dilemma of our lives—whether to subject Yogita to the harsh regimen of chemotherapy. Since Yogita could not express her pain, we would have no way of gauging her suffering.

Upon entering our home, Rachita and Rahul began laughing and playing with each other, a stark contrast to the darkness of our situation. Yogita sat on the sofa; her fever was mild and her lymph nodes were still swollen. She didn't have the same enthusiasm to play as her siblings did.

Mamatha and I retreated to the bedroom and closed the door. Mamatha began to cry again. I went to sit next to her on the bed, took her left hand, and gently squeezed it, a gesture of solidarity in our shared battle against fate.

"Mamatha, we need to make a crucial decision about Yogita's treatment," I said softly.

"Let's discuss it later, Mona. I'm too shattered to think clearly right now."

"I'll call Susan and let her know about Yogita."

That evening, Susan arrived, followed shortly by my sister Padma. They tried to console Mamatha, but their words felt hollow and inadequate.

"She doesn't have much time left, Mamatha," Padma said gently. "Keep her happy by doing the things she loves."

As the heaviness of the day's events pressed on my heart, I was drowning in questions that offered no comfort. After nearly an hour of fervent prayer that very morning, I wondered, *did those prayers mean anything at all? Could they have changed the course of fate if I'd spoken sooner? Or are they being answered in ways I can't yet comprehend?*

The past couple of years had blessed us with so much—but now, that light was eclipsed by darkness once again. Was this truly divine intervention? A way to end Yogita's silent suffering? Had Mamatha's desperate cries for mercy from a cruel world somehow been heard? The answers, if they existed, eluded me, leaving only a haunting sense of uncertainty.

CHAPTER 16

My Eyeless Angel is Gone

(August - December 1997)

Oscar Wilde once said, *"When the Gods want to punish us, they answer our prayers."*[6] In his view, we often don't fully understand what we're asking for when we pray. Our awareness is shallow, while our unconscious desires run deep, and if our prayers are fulfilled, it may feel less like a blessing and more like a punishment. We ask for things in ignorance, only to regret it later.

Deep within my subconscious, had I been praying for an escape for Yogita from her suffering?

The following morning, I awoke early and found a notepad and pen beside me on the bed. Mamatha had written down her thoughts about chemotherapy for Yogita.

> *Chemotherapy treatment: As I feel my daughter will not be able to withstand it, I let nature take its own course of time and action. I feel even if she were to become all right today, she will ultimately, within a short course of time, attain your feet. As a mother, I feel she attains your feet sooner as there is a bad, mean, cruel world out there; people are waiting like vultures, and it is not safe here. I have always worried about her when she becomes big and about her future. God, I am sure I have passed this test of yours. I have looked after her with all my best affection*

and attention too. I place my angel in your lap. PLEASE TAKE CARE OF HER

I will always be glum in my heart without Yogita.

LUV MAMATHA

To distract myself from the burden of that choice, I sat down with the pen and paper and made a list of my own of the things that brought Yogita joy:

- Going for long drives with Georgio Moroder, Fleetwood Mac, Alan Parsons Project, Ronnie Milsap, and Alanis Morissette playing on the stereo.
- Sitting beneath the warm, steady flow of the shower.
- Playing endlessly with empty cassette covers.
- Walking inside buildings, running her hands along the walls, feeling their texture with curiosity.
- Eating ice cream.

We needed to be sure to focus on her favorite things over the coming days.

On the fourth or fifth night after Yogita's cancer diagnosis, I jolted awake at midnight, my body drenched in sweat, shivering despite the warmth of the night. My heart raced as the memory crashed back into my mind—Mayo Clinic's advice all those years ago. The doctor had urged me to consider removing Yogita's eyeballs. The tumor they had detected was benign at the time, but he warned me it might eventually turn cancerous.

The thought of that conversation was haunting me. I hadn't told Mamatha the full extent of the doctor's recommendation back then. I couldn't bear the thought of putting her through that decision, of facing the unbearable truth that we might need to rob our daughter of her eyes to save her life. So, I buried it deep within myself, convinced that as long as Yogita's eyes weren't causing immediate harm, we could wait and see. But there we were, trapped in the possible consequence of that silent decision. Self-blame gnawed at my soul with teeth sharper than ever, guilt clinging to me like a shadow, unshakable, always lurking.

Yet, despite the seriousness of that unspoken choice, Yogita's calm presence after the diagnosis gave us unexpected relief. She wasn't in pain or distress; her sweet spirit remained steady, and in that stillness, she soothed us. Even as we watched the storm gather, her quiet grace reminded me that pity had no place here. Once again, Yogita was teaching me not to let grief swallow me whole.

In those early weeks, Mamatha and I slept with all three children tucked between us on our large bed, tossing and turning, cuddling them every so often. Within a month, Yogita lost seven kilograms as the cancer cells multiplied. From thirty kilograms, she was now down to just twenty-three. She had a continuous fever, with repeated infections, and began to bleed from her gums. Her lymph nodes swelled to the size of lemons.

Despite all the hardships life had placed before her, she radiated love and laughter, even in her darkest moments. It was remarkable how Yogita, in her short life, had transformed me into someone who could face the most harrowing of trials with gratitude and courage.

By early November, Yogita's condition worsened. Her breathing slowed, and her fingernails began turning a faint shade of blue. Large rashes appeared on her once flawless skin, and she scratched them until they bled. The extra doses of steroids did nothing but make her dizzy and agitated all the time. She grew more restless, unable to take more than a few steps. Sridhar advised morphine, which deepened her sleep, leaving her unconscious for most of the day.

Rachita, now in first grade, couldn't understand the sudden distance from her sister. Unable to grasp the severity of Yogita's condition with

153

her young mind, she often pestered Mamatha. "Can you wake her up, Amma? I want to play with her in the garden," Rachita would plead. "Why is she sleeping so much?"

Mamatha, helpless, would offer gentle reassurances, her heart breaking a little more each time.

In her final months, Yogita was barely eating and began passing bloody stools, her once tall and vibrant frame now fragile and skeletal. I would drop Rachita off at Tender Care, attend to the necessary tasks at my office—signing checks, meeting with finance and marketing heads—and then rush home within hours to be with Yogita. Every moment was precious, knowing no amount of wealth or power could buy me even an extra day with her.

Conflicting thoughts gnawed at me relentlessly.

If Yogita dies tomorrow, will it be a relief?

Am I wrong to even consider that?

Should I be wishing for her life to be extended, or is that prolonging her suffering?

Does more time mean a better life for her, or just a longer one filled with pain?

And what about Rachita and Rahul? They're still so young—when will they truly understand the reality of Yogita's suffering?

With Padma and Susan by our side, Mamatha and I spent every day with Yogita. Over those excruciating weeks, we watched helplessly as our beautiful daughter, once full of life and laughter, faded away.

During the last week of November, Yogita lay on the bed, her frail body swollen from the steroids. Suddenly, she went into convulsions. Panic surged through me as we rushed her to Sita Ranga Hospital, owned and operated by Sridhar. He had arranged for us to stay in a special ward just above his consultation office, a small comfort amidst the chaos.

By December, my heart ached with the brutal reality of Yogita's suffering, and I found myself wishing for her release from the agony that had become her daily existence. The torment of her pain seemed to grow heavier with each passing day. I questioned if we should have done the chemo.

To compound the anguish, well-meaning relatives offered platitudes that stung more than they comforted. "Everything happens for a reason," they would say. "Her suffering will end soon." Their words, though meant to console us, only deepened our pain and frustration. I began to understand they were grasping for something to say, unable to fully understand our anguish. What I needed most was simply their silent presence, a comforting companionship in the face of our overwhelming grief.

On the 19th of December, at Sita Ranga Hospital, at around 11:30 a.m., as Mamatha and I were changing sheets that were covered in Yogita's vomit, Yogita then went into convulsions and began making strange noises. She was gasping for breath as I held her in my arms. Suddenly, her wheezing and breathing stopped.

"Someone get my brother!" I shouted at the top of my lungs, my voice cracking as I carefully held my daughter.

Sridhar came running from his clinic downstairs, followed by his assistant, Dr. Shivu, who called out to the nurses as they hastened to the ward. Sridhar immediately took Yogita from my arms, laid her down on the bed, and started CPR, frantically trying to resuscitate her.

Yogita did not respond.

Sridhar's hands slowed, his movements steadying as reality set in. He finally spoke without looking at me, his voice low and broken. "She's gone."

Mamatha began to cry loudly as Dr. Shivu gently guided us to the hall. I stood by the entrance while Mamatha leaned on me, sobbing into my shoulder. Through the doorway, I watched as the nurses disconnected the medical devices from Yogita's body and began cleaning her with the care one might give to an inanimate object.

Dr. Shivu approached me and said, "Please collect her death certificate from the office downstairs. You'll also need to request a postmortem waiver. Then you'll be able to take her home."

I nodded in acknowledgment.

"Who will carry the remains?" Dr. Shivu asked.

I pursed my lips. "It will be me."

When the nurses finished wrapping her in a clean blanket, I lifted Yogita's shrunken, lifeless body from the hospital bed, cradling her in my arms as I walked into the hallway with Mamatha and her mother following behind. After a few steps, the sight of Yogita's two hands dangling motionless caused me to feel faint. A male nurse rushed to my side, taking Yogita from my arms and carrying her outside to the car.

As he delicately transferred Yogita's body into the vehicle, a wave of conflicting emotions washed over me. While I felt a surge of gratitude for the nurse's timely assistance, a deep sense of anguish and shame overwhelmed me, knowing I was taking my lifeless daughter back home.

The drive was shrouded in an oppressive silence, punctuated only by Mamatha's quiet tears. Once home, we laid Yogita's body in the main living room for relatives to come and pay their last respects. Yet, even in death, Yogita did not receive the reverence she deserved. As friends and family arrived, I could hear comments like, "I couldn't see Mamatha and Mona struggling to parent her," or "It will be a relief for her to be back with God."

I retreated to our bedroom, overwhelmed by a profound and desolate loneliness I had never before experienced. Even Mamatha seemed distant, lost in her sorrow. Alone, I broke down, my cries echoing through the empty room. "Why does everyone think this is a relief? Why don't they understand?" I screamed, my voice raw and desperate. It was the saddest and lowest point of my life.

We had brought Yogita home around 11 a.m., and by 5 p.m., it was time to take her to the crematorium with my brother Murthy, Ranga Swamy, and a Hindu priest. Witnessing the last physical trace of a loved one consumed by fire is meant to provide closure, a realization we will see them no longer in the physical realm. This practice is one of the significant aspects of the Hindu religion. Yet, in a disheartening tradition, mothers are not permitted to perform the last rites for their children. Reasons cited range from the belief women are too weak to endure the sight of the pyre—an outdated and sexist notion by today's standards—to the expectation women should remain at home to manage household duties while men handle the cremation. Mamatha ultimately acquiesced to these customs and traditions, despite her yearning to join me.

At the cremation ground, I felt suffocated by the reality of what was happening. I carefully placed Yogita's lifeless body on the funeral pyre, arranging her feet to face south as per tradition. I wept uncontrollably, with my tears freely flowing and my heart pounding like a drum in my chest.

Holding the earthen pot filled with water over my left shoulder, I embarked on three ritualistic circumambulations in an anti-clockwise direction—a solemn farewell around Yogita's mortal remains. I poured the water out through the small hole in the pot, symbolizing an offering to appease the transition of Yogita's soul to realms unknown. The pot, now emptied, was shattered near her head. With each step, memories of her laughter in our shared moments washed over me, intensifying the ache of her absence.

Following the ritual, I focused on the prayers for her onward journey—a wish for an afterlife filled with peace and abundance. I set the pyre alight, tears streaming down my face as I watched the searing flames envelop Yogita. The intensity of my grief reached a crescendo, the flames' fierce dance mirroring the turmoil within me. My knees buckled under the weight of sorrow, and I began to collapse. Murthy quickly came to my side, steadying me with a firm grip on my shoulder. He ensured I remained present, as the act of witnessing the last physical trace of my loved one consumed by fire is integral to finding closure. It is a crucial aspect of the Hindu tradition, reinforcing the finality of our separation. I stood, rooted in place, as the relentless flames gradually consumed Yogita's mortal vessel.

I gasped for air at the sight of Yogita's charred remains. The experience was agonizingly unbearable, and I sobbed uncontrollably. Tears flowed without end as I, with trembling hands, carefully extracted a fragment of her bone and filled a pot with her ashes.

Following a cremation, the remains of the deceased are collected and placed in an urn, then immersed in holy water on the day of the last rites or the third, seventh, or ninth day in a ritual known as *Asthi Visarjan.*

Accompanied by Ranga Swamy, I set out for Paschimavahini, a small tributary of the Kaveri River, to immerse Yogita's ashes. Standing on the riverbank, I watched the flowing water as it coursed past me, feeling a profound connection with Yogita. I released the last of her remains into the water, allowing the urn to float away with the undulating currents, carrying her essence beyond the realms of mortal existence.

My eyeless angel is gone.

As Yogita's essence dissolved into the waters of the Cauvery, I found a profound sense of solace in the realization her legacy had become a guiding light for me. Though she had no sight herself, Yogita illuminated a path of humility, compassion, patience, and tolerance—virtues I had never imagined I possessed. Through her, I learned to see life from a perspective I could not have conceived, even in my wildest dreams.

Before Yogita, I had never spent meaningful time with a blind person. When I encountered someone with visual impairment, I would look away and move on, unable to connect with their reality. Ironically, it was my blind daughter who corrected my own myopic inner vision. Until I was thirty, I had taken everything for granted.

We often disregard the importance of our wealth, shelter, family, and surroundings. Yet, when we consider what would be hardest to lose, we usually think of material possessions, rarely acknowledging the value of our senses or physical and mental health. If we and our children are blessed with intact sensory faculties, we might mistakenly believe we somehow deserve it.

But as the calm of Yogita's passing settled into the depths of my soul, a new storm began to brew within me. Little did I know, the greatest challenge was yet to come: a profound and unrelenting depression that would test every lesson Yogita had imparted, and confront the depths of my resolve.

CHAPTER 17

From the Shadows, Resilience Blooms

(1998 and 1999)

Just before leaving for home from a particularly hectic day at work a few months after Yogita's death, I received an envelope with a letter from Susan.

My Dear Mohan and Mamatha,

Please forgive me for reminding you of things you are trying to forget, but I felt I must share my thoughts. I was very hesitant to take care of Yogita in the beginning, but I do not regret it one bit. In fact, I am grateful to you for giving me the chance to be involved in her care.

Today marks exactly four months since her passing. There isn't a day that goes by when I don't think of her. At 11:40 a.m. on December 19th, the last petal of my little flower dropped. Yogita taught me so much—more than I could ever teach her. I feel like I am a better individual today, a better human being, because I have learned to have compassion and respect for the less fortunate and handicapped. This has encouraged me to reach out to them more.

Physically, I was her caretaker, but now, spiritually, she is my keeper—a silent guardian angel.

Anyone who had the chance to meet her was instantly charmed by her grace and presence. She was a very lucky child, and she had the best life possible. As parents, you gave her everything. God helped us all do our best to help her cross the bridge to His open arms. Surely, it is a relief for us, who assisted her along her journey as a team, to know she received what she needed most.

May God bless both of you, Rahul, and Rachita, and give you the strength to carry on.

Thank you. With love and prayers,

Affectionately,

Susan

Please note: *I have the diaries with me if you ever want them. They are here, and I often read them and listen to the tape. She was my only granddaughter, and she will always have a special place in my heart because of my involvement with her over the past five years.*

Suddenly, a realization struck me that I hadn't thought about Yogita at all for that entire day! *How could I forget my own child?*

The guilt of not having thought about Yogita all day felt like a betrayal of her memory. How could I allow myself to slip away, even for a moment? I wrestled with this inner turmoil all night, replaying every memory of her in my mind. Each detail of her life seemed sacred, yet time was inexorably moving forward, dragging me along.

Mamatha's parents had stayed with us for a few weeks to offer support after Yogita passed, but they, too, needed to return to their own lives. Thankfully, Rachita and Rahul remained blissfully unaware, their only concerns being occasional questions like, "Where is Yogita now?" and "Are you going there too?"

Mamatha cried every morning for weeks until she found solace in reading the Bhagavad Gita. She then decided to enroll in computer coaching classes to occupy her time and mind. As for me, I asked Susan to keep the diary with her and provide me with a summary of her experiences with Yogita, which she kindly did. I read it often, but I started to struggle with my thoughts and dreams at night.

One night, I dreamt about the talking clock we had purchased for Yogita in the U.S. The clock had a large top button that announced the time when pressed, but in my dream, it kept asking in my voice, "Does Yogita understand and forgive you for your sense of relief?"

I struggled to forgive myself. Yogita's death followed four months of intense, unbearable pain and suffering. I told myself it was human to feel a tinge of relief when the distress of watching her struggle had ended. Yet, profound shame accompanied my relief. *Was I disrespecting her by not being utterly consumed by the loss? Would she be disappointed with me or saddened I was still able to function?* I grappled with self-blame and internal turmoil. The ruminating thoughts were uncontrollable.

Was Yogita's terminal illness at such a young age due to my refusal to have her eyeballs removed, despite Mayo Clinic's warning that the tumor could become cancerous if left untreated?

Was this a form of karmic retribution or divine intervention?

Was her brief time on this planet intended to transform me as an individual?

Was she fortunate to be liberated from the misery of living in a selfish and cruel world?

As some Vedic scriptures postulate, did her soul choose this life and me as her father?

How did such a nightmare unfold on the very day I spent more than an hour praying to God?

I continue to seek answers to these questions to this day.

Philosophers argue that bad fortune exists to test good people or punish bad ones, suggesting an intrinsic cosmic meaning. They propose that suffering allows for self-transcendence. Certainly, if I hadn't endured so much pain and suffering, I would never have embarked on such a profound journey to connect with my heart.

Scientists, on the other hand, say the universe has no plans. Everything simply happens. There is no *why* or *how*. They advise not to take it personally. And finally, my religion often attributes such events to the play of past karma.

The death of parents, accidents, illnesses, and failures are like milestones in life—difficult, but easier to accept when we understand they happen to everyone. Some adversities are more complex and unique in their challenge because there's no routine way to cope with them in regular life. It's as if God sends people into the world with a disclaimer clause printed in tiny letters, like the endless pages of escape clauses in an insurance policy: *This life policy does not guarantee happiness or cover sorrows due to negligence by God.*

Providence had chosen Mamatha and me for that rare "act of negligence." My past was behind me—or so I thought—but for about a year after Yogita's death, I was consumed with paranoia if Rachita or Rahul got so much as a pimple. I knew it wasn't rational, but I couldn't stop how I felt.

True to form, my business endeavors began to slide again, alongside my personal turmoil. Arvee's outstanding loan had ballooned, with over 80 percent of that compounded interest and penal fees accrued over the previous ten years. Eventually, the bank froze our accounts. Every payment made by our customers was immediately applied toward unpaid interest, leaving us with nothing to draw from. Eventually, the bank began applying intense pressure, threatening to auction off my manufacturing facility if we did not clear the debt.

I began experiencing frequent panic attacks, with sweat forming on my forehead and my voice becoming strained and choked. A constant feeling of impending doom and helplessness followed me, which worsened to the point that I felt on the verge of breaking down whenever I talked about myself or my situation.

Sridhar informed my eldest brother, Guru, about my condition. Guru began taking me out for morning walks, listening patiently to my troubles over several weeks, though he offered no financial help.

I fought my panic attacks and anxiety with yoga, exercise, and sheer determination. Though the thought occurred to me that I might be suffering from depression, I convinced myself my mental fortitude would see me through, believing I was processing my grief.

However, even as I battled my inner turmoil, the well-meaning comments and condolences from friends, acquaintances, and family only deepened my struggles. "I know you must feel happy your child is in a 'better place' and isn't in pain any longer," or, "I know how much you loved her, but now she's free of her hardships."

Though well-meaning, these remarks fueled my inner torment. What stung most was the underlying sentiment that Mamatha and I didn't seem to be "deserving" of the same level of sympathy offered to parents who lose "normal" and "healthy" children. It felt as though they invalidated our grief over Yogita's death because of her disabilities, which deepened my isolation and added another layer of emotional pain to an already overwhelming burden.

In early 1999, after booking a week-long holiday for our family to a resort in the Maldives, we left Mysore for Trivandrum, a stopover en route. It was supposed to be a time of much-needed healing and relaxation. However, just before our flight was to leave Trivandrum, Rachita suddenly fell ill with acute diarrhea, forcing us to rush her to a hospital in Trivandrum. As her condition worsened, I started experiencing severe panic attacks almost hourly.

"Mamatha, Rachita's fever still isn't going down!" I would blurt out, my voice filled with fear.

"Relax, Mona. These things are common among kids," Mamatha, always the stronger one, would calmly reassure me.

But no amount of reassurance could ease my growing anxiety. I became overwhelmed with the fear that something terrible would happen again, as it did with Yogita. Unable to handle the mounting panic attacks and my spiraling anxiety over Rachita's health, Mamatha and I made the difficult decision to return to Mysore, abandoning the holiday we all desperately needed.

The stress of it all began to crush me. By April 1999, nearly a year and a half after Yogita's death, my body started to break down. I completely lost my appetite. My weight plummeted, and I became so gaunt that my barber even asked if I'd had my teeth removed, as my cheeks had sunk in so deeply.

Then, one Sunday afternoon, while Mamatha and I sat in the garden, the weight of everything completely overwhelmed me. I broke down, sobbing uncontrollably on her shoulder. The pressure had become unbearable, and no matter how hard I tried, I felt powerless to pull myself together.

Desperate for help, Mamatha convinced me to reach out to Sridhar, my go-to brother.

Sridhar patiently listened as I unloaded my frustrations and fears. After a while, he spoke gently but firmly. "Mona, you need to put a plan in place to resolve your financial issues. You're forty and have been through hell. I also think you're going through depression, and you need treatment. Why don't you start on medication and take it easy on yourself for a while?"

"No, Sri. It's just stress. I'm sure I can handle it with yoga and meditation," I replied defensively, unwilling to admit I couldn't handle my situation. I was hesitant to start medication. The idea that pills could alter my mind felt wrong to me. I thought I didn't need anything but my willpower to overcome what I was going through. But deep down, I was restless and unable to shake the pervasive sense of emptiness that clung to me.

Stubbornly, I doubled down on my yoga practice, convinced it was the key to curing my depression. Twice a day, I locked myself in a room and performed Hatha yoga, sometimes for over an hour. I was so determined to heal myself I would even practice my evening asanas almost naked, as if shedding the weight of everything, both physically and emotionally, would somehow restore my peace of mind.

Around this time, Murali, the close family friend who had supported me during our trip to the U.S. with Yogita, visited from Chicago. Murali had since become a professor of psychiatry at Loyola College. Sridhar, concerned about my condition, had already spoken with him about my mood swings and restlessness.

Murali spent an hour with me, observing my behavior and listening to me describe my struggles. Afterward, he suggested Sridhar arrange for a full medical examination, including blood tests, to rule out any underlying medical conditions contributing to my anxiety or depression. When all the tests came back negative, Murali sat me down.

"You're experiencing severe clinical depression, Mohan," he said, his voice steady and direct. He immediately prescribed Paxil, a ten-milligram dose of paroxetine, but I resisted, still hesitant about taking the medication.

Seeing my reluctance, Murali arranged a meeting with Mamatha, Sridhar, and my eldest brother, Guru. Together, they spent an hour counseling me, explaining how depression works and how the medication could help. Murali even played a videotape that detailed the biological and psychological aspects of depression, showing me how these medications could provide relief without compromising who I was as a person.

I began my first dose of Paxil in late 1999. By the fifth or sixth day, I noticed a slight reduction in my usual morning anxieties. It was subtle—a glimmer of hope. However, by the seventh day, I experienced strange twitching while asleep, and nightmares became a constant companion.

Concerned, I brought it up to Murali, but he reassured me, saying, "That's good news, Mohan. It means the medicine is starting to work."

By the second week, things started to shift. My appetite returned, and so did my energy. I could feel my old self slowly resurfacing—the version of me from my twenties. Sensing the positive change, I decided to increase the dosage to forty milligrams, hoping to solidify my progress.

Within three months, I felt transformed. I had energy and a renewed sense of optimism, almost like I'd been handed a new lease on life. Paxil became my lifeline, keeping my mood stable, a blessing I hadn't expected. There was, of course, a downside—it came with weight gain. I packed on an extra ten kilograms, but given the alternative, it seemed like a small price to pay.

I embraced this newfound energy and took up tennis, adding a refreshing layer to my routine. I trimmed my daily yoga sessions to thirty minutes in the morning, while tennis became my main physical outlet. The sport improved my fitness and introduced me to a new circle of middle-aged friends. These friendships were different from those I'd nurtured before—built on mutual enjoyment and a shared passion for the game.

The camaraderie on the tennis court, combined with the steadiness Paxil provided, made me feel as if I'd found balance in my life again. For the first time in a long time, I was genuinely happy.

To ease my business struggles, I leveraged a new government proposal offering interest relief to genuine borrowers and sought a one-time settlement for Arvee's debt. However, raising the settlement amount meant selling my popular food business, P&N, to the company that makes Medimix soap, then called Cholayil. Since our main food product, Vasu Puligire, was a highly successful brand, we fetched an excellent price for the company. The proceeds cleared all of my debts, settled Arvee's loans, and provided funds to drive Arvee's future growth.

I was finally debt-free! After years of turmoil, my life was finding its balance once more. From the shadows, resilience blooms. I felt a newfound sense of strength and self-worth, learning again to detach from the ups and downs of life and accept whatever came my way. Though the journey was challenging, it came with a gift of resilience forged in the fires of adversity.

Author's Note

Life rarely unfolds as we expect, and the universe has a way of teaching us to appreciate what we receive. Through Yogita, I learned the profound joy of giving more than I take. Her presence exposed me to the full spectrum of human emotions—despair, love, joy, and sadness—and from these experiences, I gained a strength I never thought possible. She taught me to strive for the best version of myself, not in search of perfection, but as an expression of the love and grace she brought into my life.

Yogita's short eight-and-a-half years shifted my perspective on happiness. No longer a pursuit or goal, happiness revealed itself as the quiet acceptance of life's mysteries and the ability to find joy in the very act of existence. Her journey made me realize that we find true contentment in embracing life in all its complexities, from the highs of triumph to the depths of sorrow. Even her passing, though deeply painful, brought with it a difficult blessing—an end to her suffering—and I have come to make peace with that truth.

Though my time with Yogita was brief, her legacy continues to shape my life. In 2002, Mamatha and I funded the construction of a room at the Rotary Yogita School for children with hearing impairment, providing accommodation for mothers and their children. A few years later, we financed a dormitory for an institution that cares for older women abandoned by their families. We named it after Yogita—*Yogitalaya.*

Today, when I visit these places, I feel a profound sense of contentment, knowing that our contributions made a difference.

Since Yogita's passing, we have donated over 100,000 USD to various charities. Now, I wish to donate a substantial portion of the proceeds from this book to continue that legacy. It brings me solace to know that, even in a small way, I can help change someone's life today.

A parent who lost a child to cancer and wished to remain anonymous once shared with me, "The joy I experience now is far deeper and more intense than the joy I experienced before I saw grief." Such is the alchemy of grief.

Because I've clawed my way from the depths of unimaginable pain, suffering, and sorrow, when joy comes—whenever it does—it reverberates through every pore of my skin and every bone in my body. I feel all of it deeply. I embrace and thank every morsel of it. My life is richer, more vibrant, and more full, not despite my loss but because of it.

I now have a new appreciation for each moment we struggled and for the courage that followed—both Mamatha's and my own—in welcoming two more healthy children into our lives, for which I will be eternally grateful. I hope Rachita and Rahul appreciate that struggles are more than challenges; they're about our growth and becoming our best selves. They test our limits, force us to adapt, and guide us toward new paths we never imagined. Challenges are the key to unlocking doors we didn't know existed.

While our physical bond with Yogita has ended, our spiritual connection remains, guiding us forward. In grief, there are gifts, sometimes many. I bow my head to each and say thank you, thank you, thank you. Because there is nothing—I mean absolutely nothing—I take for granted, and living life this way now brings me a joy I never knew was possible.

I have also learned that tragedy, though it may seem like a final chapter, is often a doorway to renewal. Choosing personal authority over the safety of collective security became the cornerstone of my self-actualization. Striking out on my own in business, despite immense struggles, allowed me to create something far greater than I could have ever imagined. Building one of the largest pharmaceutical facilities—producing a drug that helps cure millions—and creating food brands that sustained families for decades would not have been possible had I not embraced the risks, failures, and lessons along the way. These experiences taught me that when life shatters your expectations, it's not the end; it's a call to uncover hidden strengths and move forward on a new, more meaningful path.

This journey led me from a mentality of myopia to one of Amopia™—a guiding principle I've envisioned that reflects my truth: "Suffering is sacred." Embracing pain as a catalyst for growth rather than a burden reveals our true selves and builds emotional resolve. Yogita, despite all her challenges, remains my eternal beacon—radiating hope, love, and the reminder that even in our darkest hours, there is always a light leading us forward. Through suffering, we discover the strength to do more than survive; we can thrive.

Ultimately, my destiny has been to learn that true strength comes from facing pain head-on, allowing it to shape and refine us. And Yogita, with her innocence and resilience, was my greatest teacher, guiding me into a life filled with deeper love, humility, and spiritual growth.

On the cold winter night of December 19, 1998—exactly one year after Yogita's passing—Mamatha and I lay under our blankets, reminiscing about our time with her. Mamatha, her voice thick with emotion, recalled Yogita's mischievous antics, especially her fascination with flicking the electric switches on and off. As mentioned, her favorite prank was playing with the air conditioner switch, positioned just above the floor near the voltage stabilizer. On many summer nights, Yogita would switch it off just to hear the mechanical hum die, only to restart it moments later, delighting in the burst of cold air when it returned.

As Mamatha and I drifted toward sleep, something curious happened. At exactly 12:30 a.m., the air conditioner switch flicked on by itself. My breath caught in my throat. Was it the night playing tricks on us, or was Yogita's spirit playfully reminding us she was still with us? The sudden rush of cold air wrapped around us like an icy embrace—filling us with the comfort of nostalgia and the quiet possibility that she came to say hello in her own special way.

"Good night, dear Turry."

From Rahul

I felt Yogita's presence throughout my formative years, even though she passed away when I was around two. My parents often told me stories about Yogita and her significant role in changing their perspective on life. They incorporated those lessons into parenting me. One of the biggest lessons I learned from my father was to treat differently-abled people not with pity but with inclusivity and respect for the individuals they are. I will carry that with me always.

From Rachita

Though my memories of Yogita are fragmented, her presence shaped me into the woman I am today in ways I'm only now beginning to understand. After she passed, I vividly recall a friend telling me, "Yogita will always be with you," and a relative saying she had become part of the stars. I believed those words with all my heart, clinging to the idea that she was still watching over me.

While her absence left a deep void in my heart, her life gave me empathy and kindness beyond my years. I often wonder how different my life would be if she were still here—would we be best friends, sharing our own secret language? I wish I could tell her now how beautiful she was, how much we loved her despite her struggles, and how much I longed to help her experience the world through my eyes. There have been countless moments when I've felt her presence, guiding and protecting our family. Even now, I believe she's orchestrating the telling of her story, watching over us from another realm.

What if Yogita was alive?

How would it be if you were alive?
I selfishly wonder,
Would I be different?
Kinder? More compassionate?
Bitter? Sadder?
Would I have looked after you the way you needed me to?
This world never deserved you;
it always treated you differently,
like you were never one of them,
like you never fit in.
I sigh at the what-ifs,
the would-haves and could-haves,
the should-haves and ought to-haves.

But now, I will never know.
Never know how "we" would have been if you were alive.
Never know if you'd think of me as your confidant.
Never know if you'd think of me as being
your worthy younger sister.

You left us with many what-ifs,
many unanswered questions,
many nights and days when we silently wished
that you were still with us,
wished for one last day where we could
hug you tight and tell you for one last time,
"We are sorry, Yogita. We love you. It really is not you, it's them.
It's this cruel world that doesn't deserve you."

Wherever you are, I sincerely hope you are happy, you aren't judged,
you are loved immensely, you have many waterfalls to play with,
many MJ songs you can groove to.
We love you, Yogita. Maybe we just don't say it often enough
because we are scared to admit it to ourselves; we miss you,
and we miss the life that could've been with you in it.

~ Rachita ~

She lightly slipped through my fingers.
Stood there watching helplessly.
As she said "Ada" to her dad and me
One final Tata
I love you, Turry.

- Mamatha -

I Found My Pride

Betrayed and lost, I watched,
The devious plan He hatched.
A daughter born without her sight,
Leaving me shattered, with endless whys.
A road less traveled, I was ordained to follow,
Many defeats and pains I had to swallow.
I wrestled with fate, resolved and strong,
And in the struggle, I grew all along.
Though she never saw the beauty of the world,
She taught me how love and strength unfurled.
The depths of my soul she helped me find,
Her love, ageless and pure, forever entwined.
In her touch, I found my light,
Her fingers showed me what was right.
Through the darkness, she was my guide,
And in her love, I found my pride.
Her sister claps—my angel wonders why.
I shake my head, shrug, and sigh.
I may not understand His grand design,
But through it, I became fully mine.
Though fate remains a mystery to me,
Her love was my salvation, setting me free.
I'll cherish the time, brief yet sublime,
With my angel, unique, beyond time.
I know her time was far too brief,
Yet I hold no sorrow nor bitter grief.
For now, she's free, her spirit pure,
Showing the path that helps me endure.

- Mohan -

Note of Gratitude

This is my story, shaped by every experience, emotion, and feeling, true to its core. Yet, it is far from being mine alone. To claim it as such would be misleading and an injustice to those whose contributions have made it a meaningful creation.

First and foremost, I am deeply grateful to my wife and children, whose unwavering encouragement has been my guiding light. I am equally thankful for the expert guidance of my editor and publisher, Julie Colvin, and the incredible team at Wellness Writers Press.

To fully acknowledge the many other individuals whose influence has been immeasurable would require another book. I especially thank Christine Wolfe, Michelle Marie Wallace, Mohit Parekh, and Justin Foster for their remarkable support.

Lastly, this project has been a labor of pure love, dedicated to honoring the memory of my late daughter, Yogita. Her profound impact on my life inspired every word within these pages, and her brief but transformative journey continues to touch my heart and soul every day.

Mohan

Mamatha just before our wedding

Kashi Yatra ceremony

Mamatha during Gauri Puja

During our honeymoon

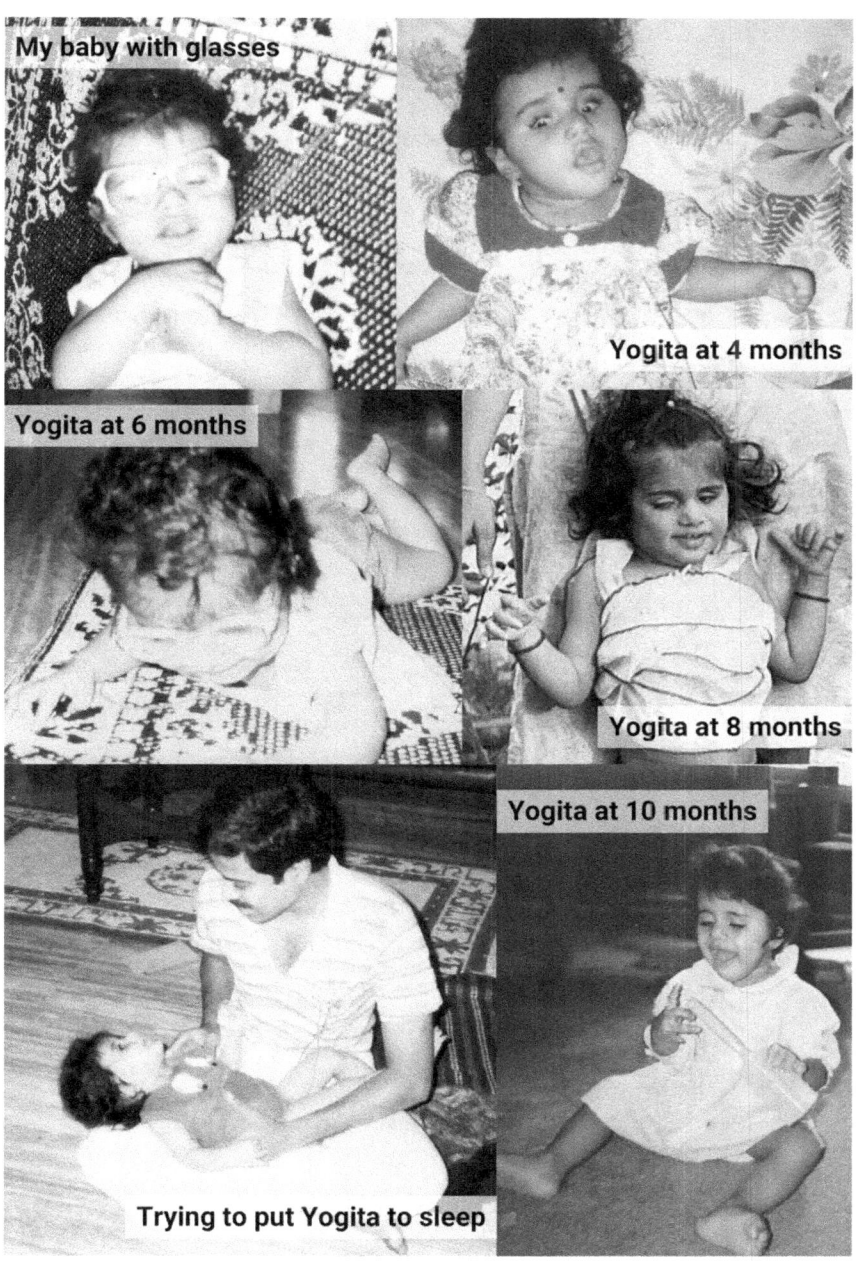

My baby with glasses

Yogita at 4 months

Yogita at 6 months

Yogita at 8 months

Yogita at 10 months

Trying to put Yogita to sleep

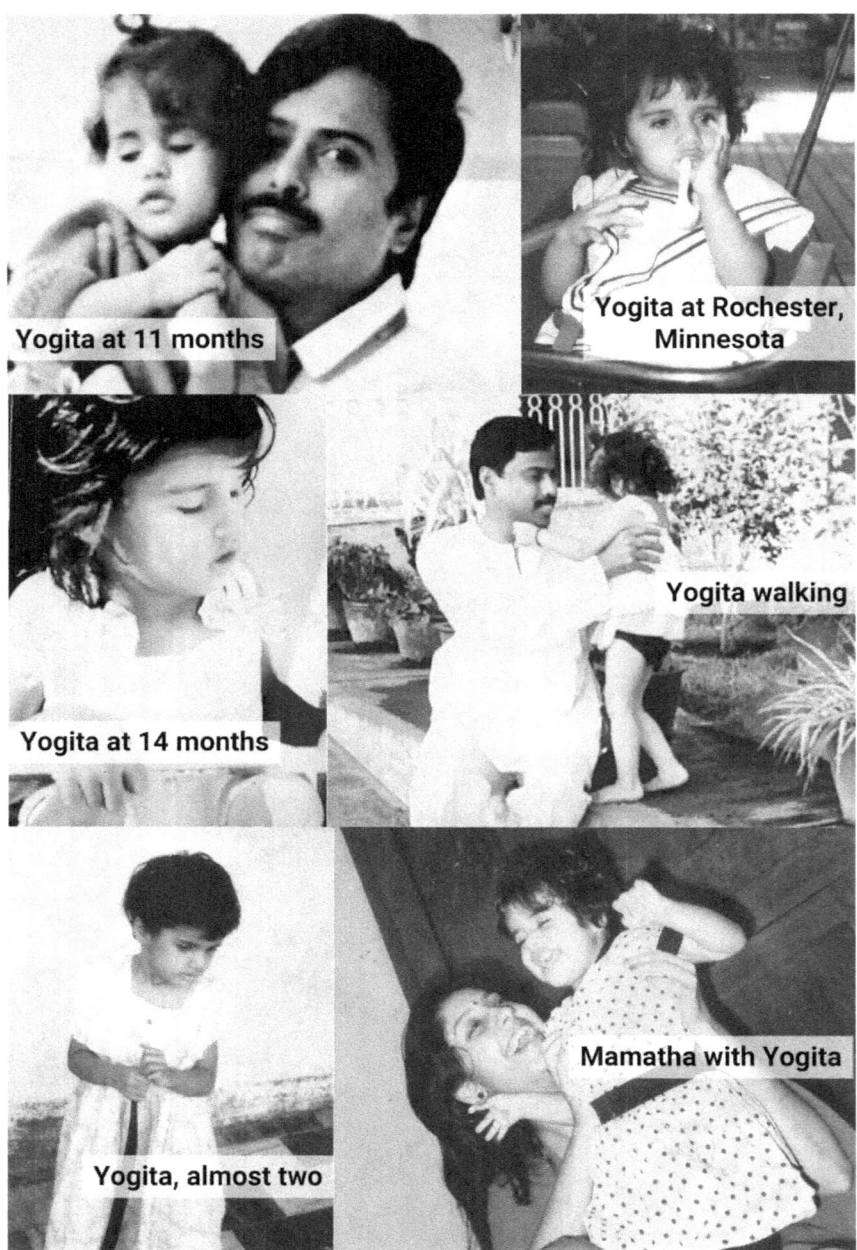

Yogita at 11 months

Yogita at Rochester, Minnesota

Yogita at 14 months

Yogita walking

Yogita, almost two

Mamatha with Yogita

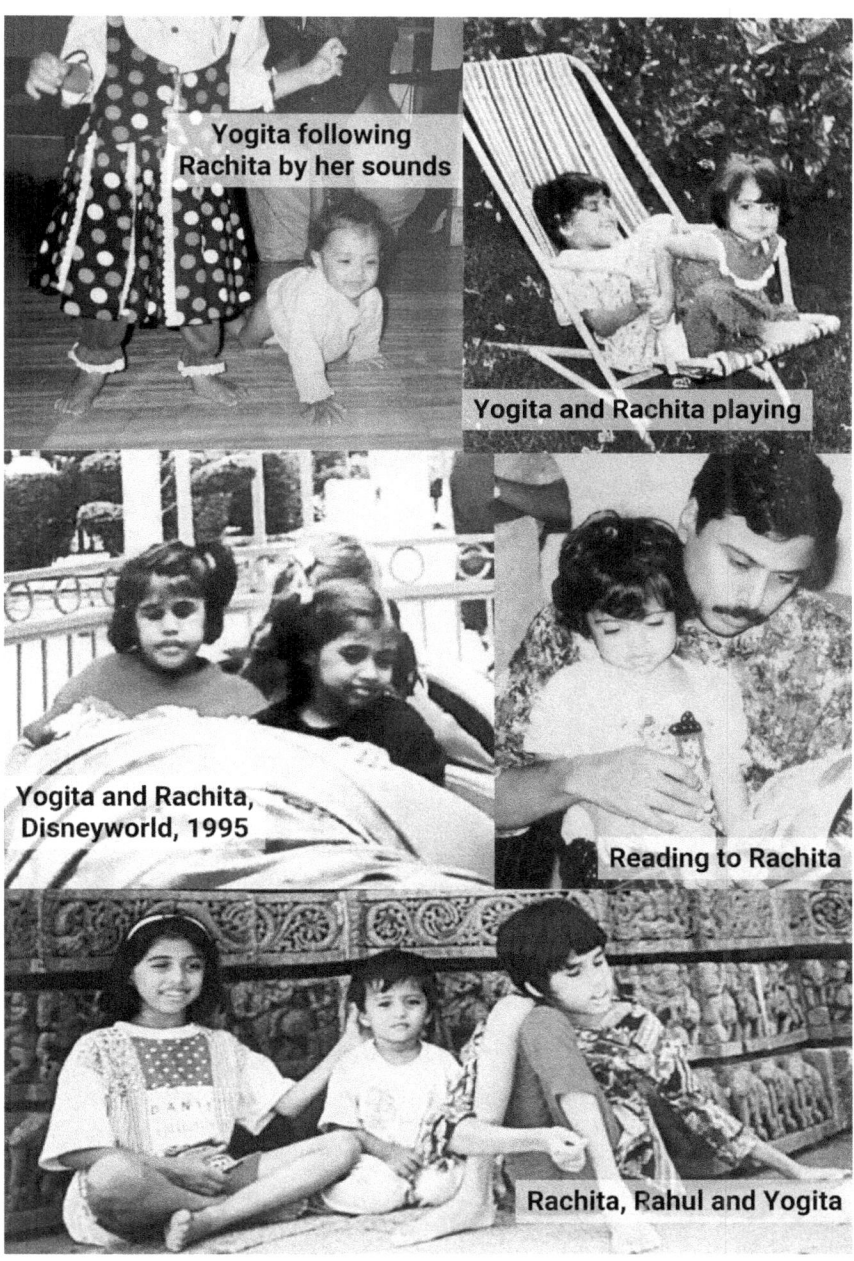

Yogita following Rachita by her sounds

Yogita and Rachita playing

Yogita and Rachita, Disneyworld, 1995

Reading to Rachita

Rachita, Rahul and Yogita

The first Hydrogenator (Autoclave) at Arvee

Construction of the Rotary Yogita School for children with hearing impairments

Yogitalaya - Dormitory for elderly destitute women

Mohan, Mamatha, Rachita & Rahul

REFERENCES

1. Leach, Penelope. *Your Baby and Child, from Birth to Age Five.* London: Dorling Kindersley Limited, 1985.

2. *Soulveda.* "Inspirational Quotes by Famous Differently-Abled Personalities." Accessed January 22, 2025. https://www.soulveda. com/happiness/no-limits-inspiring-quotes-from-differently-abled-celebrities/

3. Kingsley, Emily Perl. "Welcome to Holland." 1987. Accessed January 22, 2025. https://www.emilyperlkingsley.com/welcome-to-holland

4. Keller, Helen. *The Story of My Life.* 1903. Updated with editor Kim E. Nielsen as *Helen Keller: Autobiographies & Other Writings (LOA #378).* USA: Library of America, 2024.

5. "Helen Keller's Life and Legacy." Accessed January 22, 2025. https://helenkellerintl.org/who-we-are/helen-keller/

6. Wilde, Oscar. *An Ideal Husband.* Imprint: Nick Hern Books. Drama Classics series. Toronto, Ontario, Canada: Playwrights Canada Press, 2000.

ABOUT THE AUTHOR

Mohan Ranga Rao is an entrepreneur, explorer, and storyteller who draws inspiration from his journeys through life's triumphs and trials. A seasoned businessman and philanthropist, he has traveled to over thirty countries, seeking the beauty of nature and the growth found on challenging trails.

His award-winning debut, *Inner Trek: A Reluctant Pilgrim in the Himalayas,* chronicles his transformative trek around Mount Kailash, a sacred Tibetan Mountain. His latest book, *Myopia,* is a deeply personal memoir inspired by his daughter Yogita, whose brief life—marked by blindness and then cancer—profoundly shaped his understanding of love, resilience, and the meaning of suffering.

In addition to writing, Mohan enjoys tennis, hiking, and exploring subjects ranging from quantum physics to Vedanta. Through his work, he inspires others to embrace life's challenges as opportunities for growth and transformation.